Wild Stallion Whispering

THE STORY OF BEAR – FROM THE MOOR TO WORLD CHAMPION

DAWN WESTCOTT

HALSGROVE

First published in Great Britain in 2016
Copyright © Dawn Westcott 2016
© The photographers in respect of their
individual contributions

British Library Cataloguing-in-Publication Data
A CIP record for this title is available from the
British Library

ISBN 978 0 85704 293 4

HALSGROVE
Halsgrove House, Ryelands Business Park,
Bagley Road, Wellington, Somerset TA21 9PZ
Tel: 01823 653777   Fax: 01823 216796
email: sales@halsgrove.com

Part of the Halsgrove group of companies
Information on all Halsgrove titles is
available at: www.halsgrove.com

Printed and bound in China
by Everbest Printing Investment Ltd

Contents

THIS BOOK IS DEDICATED TO:
My husband Nick Westcott who has been a tower of strength, support
and encouragement. I am inspired by Nick's wisdom, resilience, patience,
compassion, positivity and his wonderful sense of humour.

I would of course also like to dedicate this book to Bear for the gift and privilege
of sharing life with this majestic stallion and the richness he has brought to it;
my mother Heather Williams and Sue Byrne (the breeder of Bear's mother
Collabear Countess) for their unwavering support and encouragement;
and to June Eckhart for her help and passion for the ponies.

Acknowledgements and Thanks

Dawn would like to thank the following people and organisations for their help, support and encouragement:

Nick Westcott, Heather Williams, Sue Byrne, June Eckhart, Jamie and Lisa Waters, Michael Western, the Western family, Maya Horsey, Monty Roberts, Kate Hele, Christina Willoughby-White, Julie Langrish, Sam Roberts, Suzi Roberts, Matthew Lawrence, Rodrigo da Costa Matos, Jenny Rolfe, Clive Ponsford, Margaret Quinn Evans, Brenda Lamb, Melanie Maddocks, Milly Shand, Maria Floyd and the Floyd family, Rex Milton and the Milton family, James Bryant, Kate South and the South family, Peter Green BVSc CertEO MRCVS, Sarah Bryan, Christina Williams, Ben Williams, Matthew Coldicutt, The Exmoor National Park Authority and The National Trust Holnicote Estate.

Photos: Jamie Waters – Shelduck Photography (including Cover), Nick Westcott, Dawn Westcott, Equinational Photography, Gareth Latham, Helen Disberry, Rod Smith (www.exmoor-riding.co.uk), Kate South, Rupert Kirby, Nigel Hester, Maureen Harvey, Don Hancock, Alyson Govier, Tricia Gibson, Dennis, Jay Photos, James Pyne Photos and the various helpers over the years who have taken photographs as part of their work for us.

Find out more

The Exmoor ponies, Holtball Herd 11,
The Moorland Exmoor Foal Project, Exmoor Pony Club,
Wild Pony Whispering and Wild Stallion Whispering at:
www.wildponywhispering.co.uk
www.exmoorponyclub.co.uk
email: exmoorponyclub@hotmail.co.uk
Facebook: Exmoor Pony Club; Wild Pony Whispering; Wild Stallion Whispering
Twitter: @WildPonyWhisper @StallionWhisper @ExmoorPonyClub

Chapter 1
Introduction – Born Wild and Free on Exmoor

Exmoor ponies have roamed the captivatingly beautiful moors of Exmoor National Park for hundreds of years. They are one of the oldest Native Hill Pony breeds of the British Isles and bear a striking resemblance to the ancient cave paintings depicting the little wild horses discovered by early man.

In the 1920s, a group of farmers and land owners formed a breed society and stud book to safeguard the future of the ponies. They selected an ancient-looking type – with brown colouring, black points and mealy (pale) markings around the eyes, muzzle and underbelly – to create a pedigree Exmoor pony breed from the ponies running on the moors of what would eventually become Exmoor National Park.

Exmoor ponies almost became extinct after the Second World War when reduced to just fifty mares and a handful of stallions. Their dedicated breeders have carefully nurtured the tiny gene pool and numbers have now increased to some 3500 worldwide. However, there are only around 500 free-living Exmoor ponies living in Exmoor National Park and they remain on the Rare Breeds Survival Trust's Category Two Endangered List. It is here, living wild and free in their natural, indigenous habitat of beautiful, yet harsh and challenging Exmoor moorland, that the ponies can retain their learned and genetic characteristics and behaviours – and True Moorland Type. This includes their high intelligence, independent thinking and 'wildness', where 'survival of the fittest' results in the best genetics.

The farmers and landowners of Exmoor carefully manage and maintain their small breeding herds and bloodlines and provide the ponies with the opportunity to live in natural family herds with very little interference from man. Each year, a relatively small number of foals are born and in the autumn some of them – particularly the colt foals – must leave their moorland home and find opportunities elsewhere. The foals ideally need to be sold soon after gathering, when they are easier to tame, so they can make the successful transition to life off the moors. They are wild and unhandled, yet with

Above: Hawkwell Versuvius 'Bear'

Opposite: Bear's father Hawkwell Great Gatsby running with Herd 423 on Countisbury

Farleywater H67 moorland mares running with Bear in 2015

patience, kindness and some considerate horsemanship understanding, moorbred Exmoor ponies can build a bond of trust and friendship with humans and go on to make outstanding performance ponies. However, it is not always easy to either register the wild foals or find good homes for them, which can leave some of them facing a bleak future. For decades, the foals first experience of humans at weaning time has been to endure the severely painful practice of Multiple Hot Branding on their shoulders and rumps – with up to seven large marks – as part of the registration process. Hot branding causes the equivalent of third degree human burns with necrotising lesions that can hurt for up to a week. This can result in the ponies being understandably mistrustful of people thereafter, sometimes resulting in lifelong fear and anger-based responses. In addition, when foals watch their siblings being restrained and hot branded before them, it is likely to increase their anxiety and trauma.

Hot branding of equines is now banned in Scotland and Ireland and in late 2012, the number of branded marks allowed was reduced to a maximum of four marks, applied to the rump only. In 2014, DEFRA introduced a Code of Practice for the Identification of Semi-Feral Ponies that restricted hot branding to free-living foals only. Work continues to bring an end to the practice and improve the welfare situation for free-living Exmoor ponies.

Various of the Exmoor pony herds run in the moorland enclosures comprising the Dunkery Commons (around 5500 acres) of Exmoor National Park, where Dunkery Beacon is the highest point at 1768ft. The area offers the ponies a beautiful, free-living wilderness environment.

It was into one of the oldest and most prestigious moorland herds, Hawkwell Herd 12, that a wild and tempestuous colt foal called Bear was born in 2004.

Born Wild and Free on Exmoor

Blissful, gregarious, joyful – and free. In 2004, Bear had the most wonderful start in life as a wild-born Exmoor pony foal in Exmoor National Park, which allowed him to live naturally with his mother, father, aunts and siblings.

He enjoyed family herd life to the full, born in the spring and running free on the gloriously beautiful moor until the autumn, when the pony herds are gathered in. The foals play, explore and learn with little interference from man – developing intelligent and independent-thinking minds, natural savvy and great self-awareness.

After being gathered in from the moor and passing the breed society's physical inspection, Bear was subjected to the practice of Multiple Hot Branding. Some of his six large branded marks are skewed, particularly on his shoulder, indicating that he fought hard. He was named Hawkwell Versuvius 12/223 and by all accounts his responses to being branded were somewhat explosive. His sire is the legendary moorland stallion Hawkwell Great Gatsby (bred by the Western family) and his dam is Collabear Countess (bred by Mrs Sue Byrne).

Unfortunately for Bear, despite being a fully-registered pedigree Exmoor pony foal from the long-standing Hawkwell Herd 12, no-one who wanted to buy him and his future was uncertain. He was lucky in that a local charity, the Moorland Mousie Trust, was able to take him into their scheme which helps to find foster homes for some of the unwanted moorland foals. It was there that I first set eyes on Bear – and it was clear from the look in his eyes that he was not keen to be touched by humans again.

The moor where Bear was born

The Hawkwell Herd being gathered in from the Dunkery Commons, Exmoor National Park

Chapter 2
The Arrival of the Wild Colt Foals

Three-year-old Exmoor
Harry playing with Casper
the Arabian

I already owned a lovely three-year-old Exmoor pony called Strongbow. Nicknamed 'Harry', he had first caught my eye when I'd helped with his foal socialisation.

After a career in glossy magazine publishing in London and a move to the Westcountry in 1999, I'd spent my spare time studying and qualifying in Monty Roberts' methods of horsemanship with Maya Horsey in Dorset. Monty's approach endeavoured to understand and work with the language of the horse – and Harry's foal socialisation had been part of that. I'd also helped Maya with starting horses and rehabilitating some problem horses – along with backing my own horses. Harry was now enjoying success in the show ring and I looked forward to backing him to saddle and riding him.

By this time, I thought I knew a fair bit about horse training. The wild colts of Exmoor were about to teach me that I had a very great deal more to learn.

Taking on Some Wild Exmoor Colt Foals

In the autumn of 2004, I agreed to foster some wild colt foals over the winter, effectively increasing their 'window of opportunity' to find good homes. Our small yard and barn were already occupied by the Arabian horses and Harry the Exmoor, but we had a separate 5 acre field across the lane. Although it had no field shelter, there was good hedging and the priority was to offer the colt foals a lifeline.

The Moorland Mousie Trust called to say they had some new arrivals and a friend and I went to see them. We arrived to find the barn full of foals – it had been a bumper year for colts which had put both the farmers and the charity under considerable pressure. Fillies are more easily kept in the herds or on the farms, whereas colts have to find other opportunities shortly after coming off the moor. Bewildered and fearful, the foals either stared at us or moved away behind the others, avoiding eye contact. I spotted a colt at the back whose enormous eyes met mine. He was more thickset than the others, with his front legs splayed outwards and 'rump high'. In short, he looked rather all over the place, but something about him moved me.

The charity lady pointed to a small, compact dark colt and remarked that he looked nicely put together.

'Yes he is' I replied, 'And so is that one.' I pointed at a very dark colt, with bright mealy markings around his eyes and muzzle, whose mane stood up like a Norwegian Fjord and whose eyes glittered at me with an expression that wasn't entirely friendly.

'What about him?' I gestured towards the big-eyed colt who was still staring at us.

The charity lady remarked that he looked like 'a bit of a disaster.'

I found my heart going out to him.

After looking at the foals for a while longer, she asked what I wanted to do.

'OK, I'll take three to foster over the winter, as long as you are absolutely sure they can come back to you in the spring?'

She nodded her assurance.

'I'll take that dark one with the stand up mane and that small dark one – and the one with the big eyes over there.' She looked surprised.

'He looks like a Bear,' I said. 'He might have to be called Baloo.'

After returning to pick up the colts we let down the ramp in the field and stood back. The colts blasted off to the far end and, walking up over the brow to see if they'd jumped the fence, it was with some relief that I saw three alert little faces staring at us.

'Let's leave them to it now,' I said, gazing at the large and livid hot branding wounds on their shoulders and rumps, 'They've had quite enough to deal with recently and the kindest thing we can do for them is to go away.' I could literally feel the relief emanating from the foals as we turned and walked back down the hill.

I liked the look of all three foals, but my heart was particularly drawn to the large-eyed colt who seemed to be the most wary. The words rang in my ears, 'He's a bit of a disaster.' I found myself saying to the bear-like foal, 'Baloo – no matter what you grow into, I'll love you and look after you.' I realised that already, I didn't want to return him to an uncertain future in the spring and felt our destiny was linked in some way. There was just something about him.

Shortly afterwards, winter arrived in a blazing fury and we were treated to over 6" inches of snow in November. Realising it was going to be quite some winter, we organised a field shelter. On the moors, the ponies can find myriad shelter in the combes, wooded areas, rocky escarpments, etc. Paddocks can leave ponies exposed to the elements, so providing good shelter is not just kind but a welfare requirement – no matter how hardy they are.

Top: Bear as a foal

Below: Bear with Morus and Otis

The colt foals
remained elusive.

Top: Bear is on the left

Above: Morus, Bear and
Otis

Getting to Know the Foals – Remaining Elusive

The foals were incredibly flighty and as I had nowhere to contain them they were often best viewed through a pair of binoculars. Once their shelter was built, it became a favourite spot for them but however gently I entered their field gate, they'd bolt out of it and away. It seemed that their greatest desire was to put as much distance between me and themselves as possible.

Over time, with careful approaching and retreating, the distance between us grew shorter. They became more curious and sometimes followed me as I walked away. But Baloo inevitably hung at the back, ensuring that one or other of the foals remained between myself and him.

With the other horses and ponies occupying the yard, barn and stables and the lane separating access to it, the wild colts had to stay in their field – where I was unable to separate them to progress their socialisation. As a tight little herd of three, they were formidable, as was their resolve to remain untouched.

My next plan was to build a corral where I could contain and interact with them in a smaller area. However, I didn't anticipate their reaction the first time we tested this out. After getting them used to coming into the new corral for a feed, without closing the rails, I had the impression they were accepting the space. Little did I know how important that gap in the fence was though. Because the moment I chose to quietly close the rails it was like flicking a switch. They immediately sprang into panic, flying to the perimeter where Morus, the small compact colt flung himself at the wooden rails closest to the hedge. There was a loud crack and splintering of wood as he smashed through and was off up the field. By the time I'd run towards the gap, Otis, the dark colt with the standing up mane, was out after him and Baloo was on his way. However, when he realised he would have to canter close by me to escape he sharply turned. 'Ah, got you,' I said to myself. In vain as it happened. Because he simply turned towards another section of fence, sank back onto his hocks and sprung upwards into a mighty leap over the fence, galloping off up the field after his counterparts. Forgetting the damage, I stood there open-mouthed at the sheer power and grace exhibited by the colt and pondered that, actually, no fence could keep them in if they didn't want to stay in. And this included the field perimeter fence, which was certainly no higher than the corral fence.

'He jumps like a stag,' was all I could say to people, proudly, about the bear-like colt foal.

> **TRAINING TIP:** *When you consider taking on wild foals, it's important to create the right set up. The three colt foals were simply making full use of the fact that I could not easily separate them, nor contain them. This was not their fault – it was mine. In later years, I have all of this sorted out – handling areas/corrals/pasture and the options to separate or run the ponies in herds. Back then, I was facing the inevitable outcome that 'prior preparation avoids p*** poor performance'.*

The colts slowly accepted being closed in the corral. To tame them, I would need to work with them individually, but logistically that was difficult. Despite one side of the lane adjacent to our yard offering open access to hundreds of acres of wild woodland, I decided to try herding them across to the barn, when the other horses and Harry were out in the field. It was worth a try and with a couple of helpers we managed it.

There was a stable area at one end of the barn with 5-foot high breeze-blocked walls. Next to it was another enclosure with a 10ft wide solid wooden gate across the front of it. Over the inner stable wall facing into the barn area hung a number of indoor horse rugs. This would be an ideal place, I thought, to tame the foals.

After a little hustle and bustle, it was Otis who we managed to separate into the stable. I was delighted – at last, a separated colt to work with. I looked over the door at Otis and there was something about the look in his eyes that made me feel uneasy. He walked forwards, raised himself up from his hocks and placed both front hooves on top of the rugs, peeking over the wall. A look of sheer determination on his face.

Otis and Bear as yearlings

Below: Bear

'OMG he's going to come out,' I said quietly.

'No of course he won't, it's too high, he can't jump out from there,' said my friend.

'He's coming out. Stand back,' I said. While it might have been impossible for Otis to haul himself out from that precise point, I had read his intention loud and clear and I knew instinctively that somehow, he was going to leave that stable imminently.

Sure enough, Otis, dropped down to the ground, walked backwards a few paces, then purposefully launched himself at the wall, leaping up, rocking over the top of the rugs, dropping down the other side and galloping back off up the barn to join his two comrades.

'Good grief!' was the general feeling in the barn.

I felt at once elated by the sheer tenacity, skill and ability of the colt and at the same time a sense of despondency that I still did not have a suitable enclosure in which to start taming these wild ponies.

After our helpers had left, I returned to the barn alone to see if I could make any progress with the colts, who were all enjoying some hay – together like an impenetrable little gang – at the far end of the barn.

Despite his best efforts to remain with the others, I managed to separate Baloo into the enclosure with the wooden gate.

'Brilliant,' I thought. 'I'll very gently close the gate and just stand here quietly and let him get used to being in this space with me.'

As the bolt slid shut, there was a whirring noise and feeling of energy and the colt launched at the gate from behind me, flying over it and taking it with him. Firmly bolted into the concrete wall, it nevertheless tore loose and the solid 10ft gate went crashing to the ground, while 'Baloo' cantered to join his comrades at the other end of the barn. That was the end of our session.

'You are not a Baloo, you're a full on Bear,' I said. The name stuck.

I suppose it was the shock, the energy, the force and the sheer resilience of the colts in wanting

Top: Otis, Bear and Morus

Above: Bear on the right remained extremely wary

to avoid any contact whatsoever, that radiated through me at that point. The hopelessness of my efforts, compared to their will to remain wild. I found myself welling up and sank to the ground where I sat and, I'm sorry to say, had a little cry. I was aware of the three colts watching me intently, their heads lowered towards the ground. I had a total fail on my hands and no gated enclosure. Needing to bring the horses and Harry in to their barn, my partner and I herded the colts back to their field where they galloped off up to the far end. I confess that there was a moment where I thought about directing them into the hundreds of acres of wild woodland.

'What the hell has been going on in here?' the Arabians seemed to say as they surveyed the damage in the barn that evening.

Winter became spring and my partner asked when the three still-wild colts were returning to the charity. I spoke to the charity founder who assured me that she had absolutely nowhere to put them and what was she supposed to do? So the colts stayed with us and he was less than excited about this.

Over the winter and early spring, I'd been backing Harry, now rising four years old, to saddle. He had progressed well and, just a short while after beginning to ride him, I was asked to take part in the *Discovering Exmoor Ponies* film which was a collaboration between the breed society and Exmoor National Park Authority. This involved cantering Harry on the local common, with a cameraman leaning out of the sun roof in a vehicle driving alongside us. It was a little hair-raising with a newly-backed wild-born Exmoor but we did it, albeit with me slightly raised out of the saddle on a pony only just getting used to 'canter'. I continued to show Harry over the summer and gently ride him on. Success with Harry reassured me that I was not a complete fool with pony handling and training – but the colts continued to remind me that I was no expert either.

Harry proved to be helpful with the colts, spending some time with them in their field, and showing them it was possible to interact with humans. He may have set a good example but the colts were not yet ready to take his advice and trust us.

How I Came to Own Bear and Otis

As we approached autumn, I was acutely aware that I had still not managed to get anywhere near putting head collars on the colts. I now had three strapping eighteen-month-old entire males thundering around in the 5 acre field, gleeful in their success at evading handling. They couldn't be contained in the field shelter, and although they would tolerate me being in the corral with them, they were easily capable of jumping out if they felt under pressure. It was up to me to get the environment right so I could progress their handling. I discussed the situation with the pony charity and it was decided that the small dark colt, Morus, would return to them and I would keep Bear and Otis and take over their ownership. Morus eventually went to Ireland and became a licensed stallion so his year with us had been a useful stepping stone for him. Bear and Otis had a new owner – although my partner was not quite as thrilled as me.

Attending Exmoor Pony Foal Inspections and Recognising Bear's Potential as a Stallion

That autumn, I attended some Exmoor pony gatherings and inspections and saw at first hand what the foals experienced with hot branding. As well as the forced restraint and severe pain, it seemed obvious to me that the last foal to be branded was more affected and traumatised than the first foal, who didn't know what was coming. I was assured, however, that the foals could hardly feel the hot brands as they had 'thicker skin than other equines' and they were apparently not negatively affected by the practice. We were clearly existing in parallel universes as this was not my interpretation of events, nor I believe, was it that of the foals. Sometimes, the irons weren't heated up enough and, after re-heating, were re-applied onto partially burned sites, exacerbating the pain and suffering. I could understand why Harry and the colts retained fear and anger-based responses and why they were subsequently wary of trusting humans, beyond what you might expect from their basic 'wildness'.

(Studies by both the University of Veterinary Medicine Vienna: Erber, Regina, 2012, and 'Horse Whipping Report' by Dr Lydia Tong MA VetMB Veterinary Pathologist, NSW Dept of Primary Industries – confirm pain responses and skin sensitivity in equines.)

I happened to take a photo of Bear to one inspection and it was passed around with some interest. I was asked if the colt was gelded.

'Er, no. Actually, I haven't managed to get a head collar on him yet,' I said sheepishly.

I was advised to let Bear's breeder take a look at him before I had him gelded. So a visit was arranged with the Western family. Michael Western arrived and as we walked across the field, Bear saw us and took off at an elevated trot, spinning around on the brow to face us and fixing us with his penetrating stare. By all accounts he looked pretty impressive.

'That's him,' I said. 'What do you think?'

Michael said nothing and walked quietly up the field, pausing now and again as he approached Bear, and studied him for a few minutes.

'So do you think I should geld him?'

'No.' he said. And that was that. I had a potential stallion on my hands – who I couldn't touch or put a head collar on. It was clear that I needed to get on with handling the colts.

I realised that Bear was not 'a bit of a disaster' and was actually growing into something quite magnificent. Like many horse lovers, I had grown up in awe of stallions, dreaming of galloping a magnificent mystical creature on a distant beach. But the reality of owning one was never an option. My understanding was that they were generally handled by men, often shut away in stables, treated with extreme caution and by all accounts, were a mass of fiery behaviour. Certainly not for me. Until now.

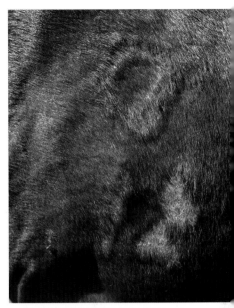

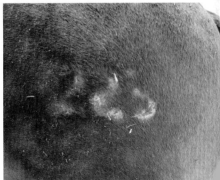

Bear has six hot branded marks on his shoulder and rump which periodically cause flaking and uncomfortable skin

Butter wouldn't melt —
but don't touch us!
Otis left and Bear right

Chapter 3

The Taming of Bear

Bear's First Head Collar

'You should take the colt to the Exmoor Pony Christmas Foal Show,' I was advised.

Held in early December, the show was only a few weeks away and Bear and Otis remained resolutely out of reach. I invested in a metal handling pen and set it up around the outside of their field shelter to create an area where the ponies could stand inside or outside. This way, I could work with them in a contained space, but without being completely shut inside the shelter with them, which would be too much pressure for them and unsafe for me. As Otis was now coming up to me in the field, it was relatively easy to separate him in the new area and over a few gentle 'advance and retreat' sessions, he allowed me to put on a head collar. He was immensely wary but was also now tentatively looking to connect with me – as long as I was always careful to be quiet, clear and patient.

The reason it was relatively easy to separate the colts was that Bear had absolutely no intention of being caught alone inside the penned area and I knew that I'd have to exercise stealth to achieve it. One day, I managed it and when he realised the pen had been closed, blocking his exit, he erupted, charging at the panels to try to re-join Otis. It was a hair-raising couple of minutes – and so important to somehow end this first session on a positive note. As soon as he paused and took a breather, I quietly opened the panel to the field and he charged out. There was no point in progressing any attempt at actual contact until he accepted being contained in the pen. This evolved as he began to accept eating a feed inside the pen with Otis, while it was shut. I could then let Otis slip out, while containing Bear. He was so wild, but had a kind look in his large, soulful eyes which gave me hope that one day he would trust me.

Bear progressed to allowing me to stand in the contained area with him, but he would not let me touch him. I wanted him to realise that this was a two-way communication and I used a careful process of advance and then retreat, pausing whenever he paused, and stepping or turning away again when he looked at me. I wanted him to understand that I would not betray him by lunging at him, or trying to grab him. I also had to take care not to 'creep' – which can look predatory. Despite these quiet, gentle interactions, he could be formidable and explosive, and I did

It took great patience to persuade Bear to accept a head collar

A milestone had been reached – Bear had accepted a head collar

Training Tip: *Nowadays, I would spend more time at liberty, working gently to move the pony's individual feet and establish the 'draw to me' – before introducing leading. This enables horse and handler to 'tune in', connect and communicate. When foals have been tied up tightly and forced to endure severe, repeated pain as their first contact with humans, this can result in fear of both ropes and handling. Somehow, we must persuade the foals that the rope is actually a friend. Establishing trust at liberty can be very effective in dealing with traumatic memories.*

my best to keep my own butterflies in check. I knew he could hurt me if he chose to attack, but I also knew that we had to overcome his fear if he was to have a good future. There was a good character inside of this magnificent and touch-resistant colt. He had not tried to kick or bite me – only move away so as to avoid being touched. After what seemed like an age of gentle interactions and pauses, he allowed me near enough to touch him briefly on the rump. It was like an electric shock had gone through him and he broke into a full sweat, from head to tail. I have never seen anything like it – before or since. I gently touched him again.

'There Bear, it isn't going to kill you.' As I said it, I realised that this was indeed what Bear had feared. That the very lightest touch was going to kill him. Or hurt him terribly.

I breathed deeply and calmly. He also began to breath more deeply and then he sighed.

'It's OK Bear, I am never going to hurt you. ' I felt an incredible protective feeling for this proud colt and hoped he understood my intention.

I took the head collar and gently worked my way along Bear's side and while he stood there frozen, I slipped it on, gently did it up, stroked him – and took it off again. Then I let him go.

A milestone had been reached. The most difficult point had been passed. Bear had allowed me to touch him at last – and put on a head collar.

Bear Learning to Lead

With much patience, Bear let me put on the head collar again in our next sessions. But he had a real problem with the lead rope. Each time I clipped on the line, he would stand there, rooted to the ground, before exploding away. There was no space to properly work on leading in the field shelter area – so this had to be done in the fenced corral, where it had become thick and slippery with mud during a recent period of relentless rain. I couldn't clip Bear onto the line in the field itself as he would have just taken off with it and frightened himself even more.

So we moved the metal pen from the field shelter into the corral to set up a smaller area where there was room to get Bear used to the rope. He needed to accept the concept of basic leading, because across the lane in our yard area was our sand and fibre schooling area where we could progress our interactions more safely. First though, I had to get him over there.

I used the Monty Roberts Dually head collar, which has a rope noseband alongside the normal noseband which tightens if the horse pulls away – and releases when the horse stops. The horse works out very quickly that the noseband tightens because he has put himself 'into pressure' – and there will be a moment of surprise where he will look to his handler. If the handler conveys a passive stance and 'releases' the pressure by loosening the rope (a long rope is necessary), the horse receives a clear invitation to re-join the handler and remove himself from the pressure. He has a choice. A normal head collar just feels like a general 'pull' on the head, which a horse in flight can resist. While I didn't want to put a horse 'into pressure' as part of normal handling, the Dually is helpful with a fearful horse that wants to explode away from you, like Bear did.

After a patient process of acclimatising Bear to the rope, I progressed to leading an extremely wary Bear across the lane to our yard. He felt like he might explode at any moment and as soon as we entered the small manege, he did. Taking flight, he tore the lunge line out of my hands and cantered off at speed around the school. I stayed calm and when he stopped, I quietly made my way towards him, pausing when he looked at me and reassuring him that I wasn't going to suddenly grab at him. When I picked up the line, he exploded away again. This time, I was ready. There was good footing and no mud, so I was able to brace and as he leapt away, the line went taught and he felt the pressure on his nose. He turned in mid-air to glance at me and I went passive, softening my stance, releasing the tension of the line, turning slightly away and trying to show him that I was inviting him to come back to me. There was a palpable hesitation. A moment of contemplation. He stopped taking flight. Then he took a few tentative steps towards me. We stood quietly together and although I knew we had a long way to go, another significant milestone had been reached. Bear had made the decision to come back to me. There was no doubt that he knew his strength as he'd broken away so many times before. This was a conscious decision to contain his power and return to me. The first tiny seeds of trust and connection had germinated.

I should point out here that I didn't use the full 'Join-Up' technique with the wild Exmoor ponies. Firstly, I didn't have a full-sized round pen. Secondly, after years of training in the practice, I felt that the wary Exmoors respond better to the method's gentle 'advance and retreat' elements rather than 'Join-Up' itself, which requires them to be 'sent away' to take flight before being invited back in to join the handler. Perhaps because of their independent-thinking, free-living evolution, a full Join-Up can be rather like shouting when in fact, they seem to respond better to whispering. The flight instinct of an alarmed wild Exmoor does not see conventional post and rail fencing as a barrier! In this respect, they are perhaps more like wild deer than horses and handling needs to ideally be refined to suit that – it truly is a process of 'gentling'.

Taking Bear for his First Walk Out – and a Big Test

A week later, I decided to take Bear out for his first walk – we did not have much time left before the Christmas Foal Show. Taking along the more experienced Harry to give Bear some company and reassurance, the plan was to walk along the lane and then the track approaching the common. We made it up the lane but as we turned to go up the track, Bear suddenly produced his explosive response, tearing the lunge line from my hands and galloping off up the track towards 350 acres of open common. We, including Harry, stood looking after him in some shock. He was gone.

Although worried about Bear, I also felt this was a crucial time to test our connection so we led Harry back out to the lane and stood quietly out of sight of the track.

'It's up to Bear,' I said. 'He has to decide what he wants now. To be with us or to be free.'

We waited. And waited. Then we heard the sound of hooves cantering back down the track.

As they approached I stepped into view and there he was, the sodden lunge line trailing behind him. He stopped a few feet from me and we looked at each other.

The colts play robustly, sometimes joined by Harry

Top: Harris and Otis

Above: Bear and Otis

Bear learns to accept leading and loading

Training Tip: *At the time, I was using a flat lunge line which is 'dead to the feel'. If you tap it, no vibration carries up the line to communicate with the horse. A decent marine doublebraid rope sends a vibration up the line which the horse can feel. This leads to more subtle communication where an intention and request can be conveyed to the horse – softly.*

'Bear,' I said, 'It's your choice. If I pick up that lunge line, you can come with me and we can see where this goes. If you don't let me, then you will have to fend for yourself because you're telling me that your future is not with me.' It was a serious moment.

I quietly picked up the lunge line. Bear didn't move and we looked at each other.

'Then you've made your decision. Let's go home.' I said.

The seeds of trust and connection were growing.

Preparation for Bear's First Outing – the Christmas Foal Show

After Bear had taken off on our first walk and returned of his own free will, things progressed rapidly with his handling. He and Otis liked to loose school together. I came to understand that wild ponies really appreciate being at liberty and learning alongside each other. Having lived wild and free out on the moor until weaning, suddenly being under the physical control of humans is not easy for them to accept. When Bear and Otis came over to the school, working with them at liberty helped them to connect with and understand my intentions and requests. It also allowed them to express their feelings. I could move their feet, ask them to turn, slow down, speed up and invite them to draw to me – and the trust started to build.

Bear gradually allowed me to groom him all over his body and pick up his feet. As long as I approached him carefully and ensured he understood my intention, such as showing him a brush before making contact, he tolerated it. Always aware of his capacity to explode, it was reassuring that his natural instinct was not to kick, bite or otherwise try to hurt me. There was a gentleness radiating from this proud, tempestuous colt that went straight to my core. Over the next two weeks, Bear learned to load in the trailer and lead nicely without breaking away. The odd mishap occurred. One morning, I was taking him for a walk up on the common and he managed to catch and step on his line, causing the clip to break – and it fell to the ground. Bear was now loose on 350 acres. He had every opportunity to take off and he knew it. We stood there looking at each other. I slowly bent down and picked up the line. The catch was useless and I had to tie it back onto his head collar with a knot. He stood there quietly and let me do it. He had chosen to stay with me. We were getting somewhere.

The Exmoor Pony Christmas Foal Show

The day of the show arrived and it was held indoors at a local equestrian centre. I had some butterflies at the prospect of taking Bear on his first outing. The judges and stewards had entered into the Christmas spirit with a variety of decorative clothing and Bear was neither accustomed to leading around an indoor environment nor being in the proximity of strangers wearing sparkling festive tinsel. Nevertheless, despite a few bursts away from me to the end of his line, we managed to stay together. It was a good first show. Bear stood Best Yearling Colt and won his Breeders/Progeny class in which we took part with Michael Western.

I received some interesting advice from pony 'experts'.

'Every pony requires a conversation at some point and the earlier it takes place the better.'

'What do you mean a conversation?' I asked.

'Well, you take him into the stable and show him who's boss. They're much better after that and know what's what.'

'So what do I do with him in the stable?' I was trying to imagine how to conduct this conversation.

'Well you show him who's boss my dear – and make it very clear.'

The penny was beginning to drop.

'Oh I see – is that what happens with your ponies?' I asked.

'Oh yes, and mine know to never step outside the stable unless asked. I don't even have to shut the door,' she said proudly.

'How did you teach them to do that?'

'Well I stood outside and each time one tried to come out, I gave it a good whack, right across the nose. Taught them in no time. They're quick learners, ' she said even more proudly.

'I expect they are,' I said.

Other methods of 'taming' ponies included shutting them in dark stables with the top door shut, tying them up to things that wouldn't break and leaving them there until 'quiet'; throwing buckets at them; whacking them with walking sticks or whatever was to hand – and even tying a leg up (hobbling) and leaving them to stumble about until they 'behaved themselves'. As these pearls of wisdom were imparted, I listened and said very little.

I knew these negative, punishment-based methods would be the very worst course of action to take if I wanted to continue to build trust with Bear and retain the immense 'sparkle' he was beginning to display.

Bear at the Exmoor Pony Christmas Foal Show – his first show

Fear and Anger-based Responses

There were already clear differences in the way Bear and Otis learned. Bear showed his apprehension through fear-based responses and a strong flight instinct. Just one mistake on my part and he was looking to break away. Otis on other hand was altogether more angry about everything and prone to defensive reactions to things he considered a threat. His tolerance of men was almost zero so a 'threat' could include the mere presence of a man. Shortly after being able to put a head collar on Otis, I wondered if there might be a particular reason for his continued defensiveness – alongside the obvious hot branding experience. On first being able to examine his mouth, I discovered that he was missing a front tooth and an area of gum above it.

'Heavens, Otis! You must have been in so much pain when that got knocked out!' It had clearly happened quite some time ago as it was well healed. The vet felt that if he was lucky his second tooth would grow normally and the gum would eventually repair (which it did). It was understandable to me that Otis was rather defensive and I was prepared to allow for and work with it.

Chapter 4
A Stallion Licence and the Show Ring

Preparing Bear for the Annual Exmoor Pony Stallion Parade

As winter drew to an end and spring approached, I decided to take two-year-old Bear to the annual Exmoor Pony Stallion Parade, held at Ralegh's Cross Inn on Exmoor each May.

Just a couple of weeks after this was Devon County Show. Then there was Royal Bath & West Show and Royal Cornwall Show, Dunster Country Fair, and in August, the annual Exmoor Pony Breed Show at Exford Show. In order to become a registered Exmoor pony stallion, Bear needed to pass a stringent assessment by two Exmoor Pony Society Judges/Inspectors and a vet to obtain a Stallion Licence. While my plan was to complete a season of showing and then present Bear for the inspection, this was not how it worked out.

We took Bear to Ralegh's Cross the day before the Stallion Parade to familiarise him with the set up. As we walked past the inn to the field, he spotted himself in the restaurant window and stopped, snorting loudly. There was a magnificent young stallion staring back at him, and Bear prepared to lunge at him. We averted adding an uninvited guest to the lunch table of some rather anxious occupants inside, and quickly marched to the field.

'Come on Bear, that was your own reflection!' I muttered. Bear had risen to his full height and I felt like I was leading a hunter stallion around the field. Tomorrow would be interesting.

The following morning, we made ready to leave. A bottle of Rescue Remedy was packed into the grooming kit as I felt a tad uneasy about taking Bear into a ring full of Exmoor pony stallions on only his second time out. All I had to do was unload him, keep hold of him, keep him out of the way of other stallions, parade him around the ring and that would be that. Or so I thought.

As we drove into the parking area, Bear started throwing himself against the side of the trailer and we announced our arrival with a loud banging and lurching of the trailer this way and that. This drew a few gazes along the lines of 'What on earth is in there!?' When we stopped, the trailer bashing didn't cease – it was a kind of methodical Thud, Thud, Thud. I opened the back door to soothe Bear and was greeted with an intense stare, before he threw himself at the side of the trailer yet again.

Opposite: Bear standing Overall Supreme Champion of Show, at the 2006 Exmoor Pony Society Breed Show

Bear's stallion inspection at the EPS Stallion Parade

'There there Bear, it will be fine,' I lied. I went to the car to drink a quantity of Rescue Remedy.

'OK, you can let the ramp down, I'm going to bring him out now,' I said. Bring him out? Having the sixth sense to step smartly to the side, Bear left the trailer, sailed over the ramp, hit the ground, bounced and did the most fantastic Capriole. Then he stood and looked about. Miraculously, he was still on the line and we were together. There were a few mutterings from some nearby spectators and that was the first day, I believe, that Bear started to think his other names might be 'Oh My God' or 'Jesus Christ'.

'Rather you than me,' said an amused voice. I glanced around to see Bear's breeder grinning at me.

That first Stallion Parade was exhilarating and hair-raising. Bear behaved with dignity some of the time and made everyone well aware that he considered himself to be the business - producing the odd full rear and various leaps. At that time, some stallions were awarded £60 Premiums by the judges and I was delighted to be awarded one for Bear. Leaving the ring, Bear felt like a canon about to fire and I couldn't wait to get him back to the trailer, relieved that it was over. As we walked towards our sanctuary, a society official came up and told me that, although it was somewhat unorthodox, the judges had asked if I could please bring the colt back into the ring for a stallion inspection.

A stallion inspection right now? Bear hadn't yet completed a showing season so had no track record other than the Christmas Foal Show. I wondered why the judges had asked for this. However, I found myself agreeing and led Bear back towards the ring. Already rather 'lit up' after the parade, it was a big ask for him to go back in on his own, surrounded by spectators. The judges were waiting to examine Bear. He would need to stand quietly and let them take a good look at him and probably touch his legs, feet and mouth. The inspectors were careful and quiet and Bear fixed me with his intense stare.

'What the hell is this?' he seemed to be asking.

'This is very good for some of your body parts Bear, just hang in there (literally) and be calm,' I tried to convey to him. 'And don't kick or bite the inspectors please.' There was a hairy moment when one of the inspectors examined Bear's back end and I remembered to breath deeply, trying not to notice that Bear's ears were laying somewhat horizontal.

'Hold Bear,' I conveyed to him, 'just like in Braveheart'. And somehow he did.

The inspectors confirmed he had passed his stallion inspection (subject to a vet check, which Bear would later pass with flying colours). It was a thrilling moment. The walk back to the trailer was less thrilling and it was with considerable relief when he was safely loaded. I was now driving home a licenced stallion. I later found out that a judge had said that the colt should not leave the field without a stallion licence as there should be no risk of him being gelded. Bear was already causing quite a stir.

Devon County Show

At two years old, Bear was quite something to show in hand. If anything spooked him, he'd start to take flight. We'd established a kind of 'emergency re-connection' when this happened. I referred to it as V1 – in aircraft language. You still have choices before V1 then you're committed to flight. As Bear began his flight response, I had nano-seconds to convey to him that it was better and safer to stay with me. This involved a short tug-tug on the line (not a pull or he would simply pull away completely) and an invitation to come back to me. I had about three tug-tug opportunities in quick succession, along with the invitation to change his mind. It was essential that I tried to remain calm at these times. Staying with me had to represent a place of safety. If Bear read an adrenaline-high state in me, there was a greater chance he would choose to go somewhere else.

At Devon County Show the Exmoors are shown very first thing in the morning. The show ring is large, with four classes going on at the same time. That year, the Percherons, in all their plumage, were adjacent to the Exmoors. There were no boundaries between these classes, each breed had to stay within its allocated space – handlers must not let go or there could be chaos.

I brought Harry along to show in the adult Exmoor class, so Bear had to stand in the busy collecting area beforehand with my helper. Harry did very well, achieving second place in a large class of stallions, mares and geldings. By the time I had swapped Harry for Bear, the other youngstock entries had already reached the Exmoor ring and were starting to parade for the judge. Bear and I trotted in across the field and he felt formidable as he powered past the Percherons with his eyes on stalks. He saw the Exmoors and gave out a piercing call. This caused the Exmoor judge to wheel around and look at him as he offered a beautiful trot. He could certainly catch the judge's eye. All I had to do was hang onto him.

Two-year-old Bear standing Devon County Champion Exmoor 2006

Bear won his youngstock class and it was a thrilling moment when he was called forward as the Devon County Champion Exmoor – his first championship. But at this moment he also produced the first demonstration of an interesting 'quirk' when being called out from the line-up. He started to slowly walk backwards. Youngsters can find reassurance in the line up among the other ponies and they naturally don't want to be singled out to walk towards the judge and stewards. 'Backwards' is often the direction a pony will choose when uncertain – because it is the direction we least often ask them to go in, and they can therefore retain it as 'their direction'. Fortunately, Bear walked forwards again to be awarded the championship, but as the *Horse & Hound* photographer took his picture, I was aware of a commotion behind us. 'Exmoor pony loose!' announced the commentator over the tannoy. An Exmoor had gone tanking off across the ring chased by her lunge line – and Bear felt very much like he was about to follow her. There was a 'moment' but he stayed with me. That could so easily have been us. I was proud of Bear.

In the early years of showing Bear, I made plenty of mistakes and I felt that one of them was sometimes using the heavy 'stallion bit' which is *de rigueur* for Exmoors. This is a chunky straight metal bar with two large decorative metal side pieces. It sits across the stallion's jaw with a chain underneath and if the stallion pulls away or leaps about, the resulting jarring on the jaw is likely to cause bone ache, however gentle the handler tries to be. Rather like tapping a hard object continually on your shin bone – or banging your elbow. It took me a while to realise that what was going on in his mouth contributed to his tension and to change to a light loose ring snaffle. Eventually, I would come to realise that he did not need a bit at all.

Top: Otis had a Book of Rules which were non-negotiable

Above: Bear standing champion at Royal Cornwall Show 2006

Otis's Book of Rules and Gelding

After some deliberation, as Otis was also a stunning colt and had important bloodlines, I made the decision to geld him. Keeping two stallions was just not feasible. I had progressed a workable relationship with Otis based on black and white rules. These rules were his not mine. Things were either acceptable or they were not for Otis. There were no grey areas. There was no margin for what he considered betrayal or unfairness, on any level. 'Mistakes' resulted in defensive behaviour and he was fully aware of the tools at his disposal – teeth, lunging, the power in his back end and a wide range of very clear facial expressions that left the recipient in no doubt of his feelings. However, I loved him dearly and he seemed to know this. We had made a heart connection and if I was careful, clear, kind and consistent, he would let me handle him – and even show softness. Trust was slowly building but that trust did not extend or transfer routinely to anyone else. For Otis, each and every person would have to meet with his expectations and abide by 'The Rules' or the situation would be non-negotiable. But he was progressing and we were communicating.

So the prospect of gelding Otis was rather serious. He would be well capable of fighting his way through a sedative and I asked the vet to please also apply a generous amount of local anaesthetic around the testicle area. Pain can still be experienced through a sedative and I wanted to make sure there was no chance of him feeling anything at all. Once he was dosed to the nines, the vet began. Although apprehensive, Otis rested his head against me and I stroked him through the whole process, reassuring him and trying to convey that this really was in his best interests. The operation went well and he made a good recovery with plenty of pain killer for the next couple of weeks.

Triumph and Disaster

Bear's showing success continued with winning the Exmoor Championship at Royal Cornwall and the youngstock championship at Dunster Country Fair. The Champion Exmoor there was the beautiful stallion Collabear Campion Barle 'Ted', sired by the legendary Hawkwell Cock Robin – who is Bear's grandfather. Ted was shown by Michael Western, whose family own the Hawkwell Herd, and this was to be Ted's last show before his breeder, Sue Byrne, retired him. So it was an honour to be in the ring with them – and also an opportunity to see how to properly show a pony!

The disaster was a trip to a large 'up country' show. On arrival, the staff on the gate were examining the passport of every horse and pony arriving as well as the equines in their transport.

'Ooh, I wouldn't go inside there if I were you.' I said to the lady already bustling into the back of the trailer. She ignored me. I could see the flickering of Bear's ears.

'I REALLY wouldn't go in there – that is a wild-born Exmoor stallion.' Well, technically, he was still a colt but I had to say something meaningful that would avoid a Trailer-Based-Capriole.

This resulted in rapid reversing by the lady in the nick of time. A disaster averted. Unfortunately, the next one would not be. There was a long wait for the class as the judge had been delayed. It eventually started and in the ring was another Exmoor stallion. Producing a couple of leaps, Bear managed to get his front leg over the lead line, running it taught under his knee. He leapt backwards and, as I couldn't do the usual tug-release communication, was soon at 'V1' and then... free. He made a beeline for the other stallion and there were some gasps. There was no time to delay as they squared up for a confrontation, so I walked up to Bear, picked up the end of the line and invited him back to me. He came away. No damage done. However, it was enough for the judge to eliminate us and I was directed to stand at the side of the ring while the class was judged. At the end he came over and told me that I had given him 'just the excuse I was looking for'. It occurred to me that perhaps not everyone was delighted with the arrival of Bear on the showing scene.

Onwards and Upwards – the Exmoor Pony Breed Show

Held in August, the Exmoor Pony Breed Show at Exford Show is viewed by many as the pinnacle of the Exmoor pony showing year with well over a hundred Exmoor ponies exhibited from across the country. A Breed Show Championship is much coveted. I decided to take both Bear and Otis. Preparation with Otis had been coming along well and this was to be his first outing. On the day of the show, we left Bear at home as his class wasn't until the afternoon – and took Otis along for his early morning gelding class. My goal was simply to see if I could get Otis acclimatised to a show atmosphere and into the ring – and I had no thought of rosettes.

It was windy and after a long stare at the fluttering rope around the ring, Otis shot inside and we had a rather lively walk around. The flapping marquee almost brought our showing to an abrupt end for the day, but we stayed attached to each other. Nevertheless, he had caught the eye of the judge as we were called in first, and he did look incredibly dark and shiny, with vibrant mealy markings around his eyes and muzzle. Thankfully, he allowed the judge to walk around and take a close look at him without pulling any cautionary faces. The 'trot up' could be described as animated, with a super swerve past the judge showing a promising half pass. Fortunately, she still liked him. Delighted with our first place rosette in the youngstock class both Otis and I were looking forward to leaving the ring. However, the steward reminded us that we were required to stay in the ring for the Championship. Although still rather lit-up, Otis led around once again, this time with the winning adult geldings. It was both a shock and a delight when he was called forward as the Breed Show Gelding Champion. We were handed a sash along with the champion's rosette. Otis gave the sash a wild stare and started leaning away from it like a motorbike on a bend. A fellow competitor advised me somewhat impatiently to 'just put it on him'. However, one look at Otis's expression conveyed to me that Putting On Sashes was currently written in Red Capital Letters on the Unacceptable Requests page in his Book of Rules.

'Er, I think I'll wear it,' I said, hurriedly adorning myself with the sash.

Otis posed for his photo call and we returned to the trailer – we'd completed our first show and he'd stood champion to boot. It was now time to take him home and bring Bear to the show for his afternoon class.

Top: Otis was rather animated in his first showing class

Below: Otis (Boy Harry) Gelding Champion, 2006 Exmoor Pony Breed Show

'Well that's made my day, what an achievement for Otis.' I said on the way home, 'I don't expect anything from Bear today – we'll just enjoy the class.'

Returning to the showground, we had a while to wait for Bear's two year old class and so Bear and I watched the preceding classes from the collecting area. Also taking it all in was the owner of a stallion who had been distractedly clicking his fingers on the catch of his pony's lead rope. An 'Oh Dear' was muttered as he mistakenly unclipped him. Realising that he was now loose, the stallion lurched away and then curled around and made a beeline for Bear. My helper ran forwards waving her arms to turn him away, after which he trotted purposefully towards the rings and some enticing-looking potential conquests. After some drama he was reunited with his relieved owner. This had put a distinct spring into Bear's step and was a cautionary reminder of why it's so important not to let go of a stallion if you can help it. My fingers tightened on Bear's lead rope.

Soon the two-year-old colts and fillies began to enter the ring from a busy narrow walkway which ran along the hedge. In it people stood spectating, sometimes accompanied by ponies and children. It was not the best place to be taking an excited colt with a 12ft span in his Capriole. I decided the best way to navigate it without mishap was to trot its length and, as we entered the ring, the steward advised trying to hang onto Bear as we flew past. Bear gave out his mighty call, which was already becoming deep and commanding, and the judge turned and stared as we managed to slow to a walk. After joining the line of ponies there was an uneventful circuit or two, until the adjacent ridden class began cantering towards us with just one small rope separating the classes. Bear raised himself majestically onto his hind legs, high into a rear, and stayed there.

'Come down Bear – please,' I beseeched him. He came down and we moved on swiftly, with me receiving a bone-shuddering butt in the hip as he shifted his energy sideways.

'Another trip to the chiropractor – thanks Bear,' I tried to maintain a relaxed and pain-free look on my face.

Somehow, it all came together because Bear won the class, then the Youngstock Championship and then the Overall Supreme In Hand Championship. The day was incredible and I simply couldn't believe it was happening. It was then time for the Supreme Championship of the Breed Show, which included the Ridden Champion and, looking at the beautiful ponies in the ring, I was sure that Bear had gone as far as he could go that day as a two year old. I was thrilled with him. When the steward gestured to the Supreme Champion to come forward I smiled and looked to the side of me to congratulate the winner. However, the steward gestured again and the judge asked us to step forwards. It was Bear. The feeling was amazing and, of course, Bear started walking backwards.

'This, Bear, is not the time to pull that stunt – come on!'

There was no question of him not wearing a sash, so collective breaths were held as one was carefully eased around his neck – and sighs of relief as he accepted it. Yet more sashes were awarded and as one of them was for the Moorbred Championship, I asked the steward if the judge could please award this to Bear's breeder's family. Although a deviation from the normal procedure, this was duly done and it was a special moment when Mrs Anne Western came into the ring.

With Bear safely back in the trailer, I went to collect the array of lovely trophies for Bear and Otis. It was an incredible day and one I will never forget. However, I was quickly brought down to earth with a bump. 'You'll feel the chill wind now you've got a successful stallion and won the breed show.' I was told by an Exmoor pony friend.

'Why?' I said.

'Do you know that some people spend their whole lives trying to win the breed show? You've done it already and with a stallion.'

I was genuinely perplexed. 'This is an endangered breed. Surely they'd be glad to see a good stallion appearing and someone willing to become a breeder? Surely encouraging people to get involved is what it's all about?'

Above and opposite: Bear stood Overall Supreme Champion of the 2006 Exmoor Pony Breed Show

Chapter 5
Backing Bear to Saddle, Showing and Shenanigans

Some Personal Turmoil

After Christmas in late 2006, my partner decided to move back to the North and this meant that I was left care-taking our smallholding which resided some 1260 ft above sea level on Exmoor, in what can only be described as a 'frost pocket' – albeit a beautiful one.

Winter could be brutal – arriving in October and finishing after flourishes of April snow, as late as May. Now on my own, I was managing to hold it all together. Not too badly either for someone who had a background in London glossy magazine publishing and who had been nicknamed 'Barbie and her ponies,' by various of the less well disposed.

Preparing to Back Bear to Saddle

As Bear was already a strapping young stallion, I was strongly advised to 'break him in' – or back him to saddle as a three-and-a-half year old, if I intended riding him. There appeared to be few wild-born ridden Exmoor stallions, and it was a popular belief that men should handle them and they weren't for riding. However, I had a dream. I wanted to demonstrate that Exmoor stallions could be happily ridden as well as covering mares. Although Bear remained formidable, I felt it was an achievable dream and advisable to back him very lightly before he met the mares.

To progress Bear for riding, I had to get him used to the saddle and long lines. He was already familiar with a bridle and bit from in hand showing. He now needed to understand what the 'pressure' of a heel, seat and hand was all about, accept someone on his back, and allow a girth to be done up pretty tightly around his stomach. When you think about it, it's quite amazing that horses let us ride them at all.

At this point on my horsemanship journey, I still assumed that a horse needs a bit in his mouth to

Loose schooling Bear and Otis proved to be an excellent way to progress with backing Bear to saddle

Top: Bear getting used to the feel of a saddle at liberty

Above: On the lunge

back to saddle, and certainly where a stallion was concerned. However, I did appreciate the benefits of doing much of the preparatory groundwork without clipping directly onto the bit. Instead, I used the Monty Roberts Dually head collar, which can help a horse learn to steer and stop without putting pressure on the mouth – and allowed me to introduce contact on the bit gradually.

Strengthening the bond of trust between us through liberty connection and loose schooling would be key to Bear accepting all of these new things. By loose schooling, I mean a gentle, interactive process, where the ponies are asked to move away and invited back to me in a way that builds connection and trust. It's not about 'making them work' or 'dominating' them – rather exploring two-way communication where how they express themselves and relate to me is very much part of the session.

Introducing a Surcingle and Long-reining

I wanted to run the long-lines through something to stop them dropping to the ground, so the first item I introduced to Bear was a lunging surcingle. Lighter than a saddle, this would also get him used to something doing up around his middle. Once I felt he understood the feel of the surcingle, I unclipped the line and let him explore the feeling – at liberty and free of restraint. His response was to buck. As he had chosen to do this himself, I remained calm and unconcerned and let him work it out. When he stopped, I invited him to come to me and we paused and had some moments of contemplation. Then I asked him to walk around at liberty again. This time, he accepted the surcingle, so I invited him in and ended the session. Ending each session on a positive note was imperative. In the following sessions, I could feed the long lines through the rings at the sides of the surcingle, and let Bear get used to circling around me and for me to walk behind him holding the lines. He was quickly able to understand steering, stopping and moving on again. Soon he could navigate figure of eights.

Introducing a Saddle and the Emergence of a Phobia

Once Bear was comfortable long-lining using the surcingle, it was time to introduce a saddle. I used an old saddle, where it didn't particularly matter if anything happened to it. Some ponies don't buck at all during the backing process, but with Bear's responses so far, it seemed likely that he might. I carefully introduced the saddle and once he was happy I did up the girth, hole by hole, with breathing space in between. It would have to be secure as I wanted to let him explore the feel of it at liberty and a loose saddle can easily slip underneath the belly and cause panic. I unclipped Bear and after wandering around for a short while, he suddenly gave some impressive bucks. Although spectacular, Bear was not panicking and was soon walking and trotting around calmly in his saddle. I invited him in to me, removed the saddle and ended the session. At the end of every session, we spent some quiet time before I took him back to his field. It was progressing well. Soon Bear became accustomed to the saddle with the stirrups dangling down at the sides and I also started to lean over him and stand in at his side, stroking him over his rump and over the top of the saddle, which he accepted well – as long as I stood on the ground. However, when I placed a portable mounting block beside him, it became clear that he was highly sensitised to anyone standing up in his peripheral vision. This was more than basic wariness, which I'd also experienced when backing Harry to saddle - Bear was terrified of it.

What Could have Caused Bear's Fear?

During hot branding, foals are surrounded by strangers who apply restraint and Bear would have had plenty of opportunity to associate the proximity of people with the pain of being burned with multiple red hot irons. This fearful memory would be heavily imprinted in him and if he had seen his siblings hot branded before him, that could be exacerbated. This could well have triggered an understandable fear of humans standing over him and in his peripheral vision – which would have to be overcome.

As I continued with loose-schooling, long-lining, leaning over and walks out in hand, everything progressed well – except when I made any attempt to stand on anything to lean over. At this point he would become rigid with tension and move away. It was the same when I stood at his head reassuring him and a helper leaned over. It was perplexing. Some trainers use 'flooding' techniques to 'desensitise' horses to things they don't like – repeatedly applying the stimulus that concerns them until they stop reacting to it. Like tying tarpaulin to them, or flapping something at them. I knew that to use pressure-based techniques like this with Bear would be disastrous. We had to progress gently and to take the time it takes to build the solid foundations of trust. There were no 'quick fixes' – force and coercion would not work with Bear.

Bear Meets Boris

Given Bear's resistance to accepting anything in his peripheral vision, I wasn't yet prepared to get on him or put anyone else on him, because I sensed what would happen. It was likely that he would explode. So I constructed a dummy rider out of an old overall and stuffed him with hay. His name was Boris. First of all, it was just a question of getting Bear used to Boris approaching and moving out again. He gradually accepted this strange new 'person' standing at his side, waving his hands about and stroking him, then leaning over his back and coming off again, on both the nearside and offside. Boris then began to sit on Bear, but he had to remain slumped forward. If he started to sit up, Bear tensed and moved away. With gentle, progressive work over a few sessions, Bear was able to cope with a helper walking alongside holding Boris sat up in the saddle, while I led him.

After all this patient preparation, it was time for Boris to be tied on so I could ask Bear to walk on his own with his 'rider' onboard. I'd done everything I could to prepare him – and taken time to do it, ending on a positive note after each short session. After tying Boris on, everything looked good so I quietly asked Bear to move out to walk in a circle around me. After a few steps, he took off. Well more accurately, he erupted – bucking and then galloping around the small arena as fast as he could. He tore

Below: Bear learning to accept long lines and steering

Bottom: Long lining over poles

the lunge line out of my hands (another good reason for it being clipped onto the Dually head collar and not a bit) and banged Boris against the fencing. Within a fairly short time Boris started to disintegrate. While this was going on, I stood in the centre of the school with my helper and we tried to remain calm and unconcerned. Not easy with Bear's incredible reaction going on – but finally he stopped. I breathed deeply and the three of us just stood there. I gently approached him and could see that he had deep furrows above his eyes in an obvious anxious frown. He looked like he could cry and my heart went out to him. I stayed calm, quietly removing what was left of Boris, and gave some deep sighs. So did Bear, at first so tense and then starting to breathe more deeply. I wanted to convey my warmest, calmest feelings to him. He knew that what had happened wasn't right but he couldn't help himself, he was working through a gripping fear. There was no need to make anything of it, that was the last thing he needed. Neither admonishment nor over-fussing. Just the reassurance that all was now calm. After this, we walked around the school, picking up the pieces of poor Boris. I was heartily glad that I'd chosen to use a dummy instead of a person. Interestingly, Bear followed me of his own accord, staying just behind my shoulder, his head lowered – watching everything. He wanted to stay with me.

The Arrival of 'Mark from the Household Cavalry'

It's vital that any training session, particularly during backing a horse to saddle, ends on a positive note. This was not positive. So we needed to continue. It took a while to reconstruct the dummy, during which time Bear remained with me, calmly watching everything. It was only fair to get another rider as Boris was in no shape to continue, so this one we named Mark from the Household Cavalry. Mark had the added benefit of a hard hat, well-stuffed gloved hands and a body protector. He had altogether more substance. Bear stood quietly as we gently tied Mark on and we were ready to try again.

'Gently now Bear please,' I said as I carefully invited him to step around me in a circle on the lunge line. My heart sank as he took off again. Oh dear, I thought. However, at about a quarter of the way around the school, he changed from a flat out blast, to turning to glance at me. At that precise moment, I acknowledged his hesitation, dropped my shoulder and invited him to come to me. He stopped and then walked slowly towards me. Somewhat apprehensive but trying his best. I could see he was battling his fear and really wanted to try to do the right thing. We stood together and I conveyed to him that this was really good. I asked him to walk out from me again and this time he did it. We did a few quiet circles in each direction and ended the session on a more positive note than I could ever have imagined. Bear was very proud of himself. He had started to overcome his terrible fear – and he knew it. We had done this together and he had trusted me. A cup of tea was in order – and perhaps something stronger!

Mark was a confident but rather erratic rider, lurching about as Bear moved, despite being tied on pretty firmly. This was because he was unable to take responsibility for his own balance, being stuffed with hay and not having a proper skeleton. So Bear learned to accept and deal with, quite frankly, the most awful rider. When I was sure that he was happy to carry Mark – in the school and out on walks,

'Mark from the
Household Cavalry'
riding Bear

I swapped him for my helper. During the process of backing Bear to saddle, I was his place of safety, and with each new request he watched me intently. I knew I had to remain on the ground until I could transfer that trust into the saddle. I had to be where he could see me – not least so that if he leapt away, I could draw him safely back to me.

Getting on Bear for the First Time

For my brave helper to sit on Bear, we wanted to set ourselves up to succeed so decided to try it on a nearby forest track with a fairly steep, long incline. Here we had somewhere to go and something interesting for Bear to focus on – rather than just being in the school. When the moment came, we were careful to breathe calmly and my helper stood at Bear's side, checked the girth and prepared to mount. He fixed his eyes on me and allowed her to put a foot in the stirrup and lean over. Then a leg over and finally, in the saddle, where she remained relaxed and leaning forward and downwards so as not to immediately sit up straight in his peripheral vision.

'Good boy Bear, let's carry on walking now shall we. We'd like to ride you for a while.' Off we went, Bear never taking his eyes off me as I did my best to feel as though we did this every day. He accepted his rider and she gradually sat up in the saddle. After walking a stretch of track, we stopped and she slid off. Bear's demeanour during the ride was one of surprising calmness – at last, someone on his back who could balance for herself and who remained nice and still, moving with him. Mark from the Household Cavalry had done a wonderful job – Bear actually appeared relieved to swap him for a human rider.

This exercise was repeated regularly over the next week, with the riding phase lengthening a little each time. One day, when we were coming back along the lane, I gently unclipped Bear from the lead rope and walked alongside. My helper was able to ask him to stop and then proceed with gentle aids. I dropped back slightly as Bear put his focus on her and accepted her requests. At that point, I knew I could get on him myself. The following day, I rode Bear for the first time and he felt amazing. No tension, no sharp spooking. Just an incredible feeling of warmth and comfort. Already I knew this stallion was going to be exciting and wonderful to ride - and I felt safe. We rode Bear on for about a month before turning him away. He was only three years old and although strong in stature, not ready to go into regular ridden work. I had wanted him to willingly accept a rider before he started to cover mares, which would begin the following spring. For the time being, he was still living with Otis.

Showing and Shenanigans

At three years old, Bear was maturing beautifully. After another appearance at the annual Exmoor Pony Stallion Parade, his first show was to be Royal Bath & West. Competition was stiff with some forty Exmoor pony entries. Bear won his class and went on to stand Champion Exmoor. He had now won championships at all three of the main South West County shows – including Devon County and Royal Cornwall, as well as standing Supreme Breed Show Champion.

Not the Way to Greet a *Horse & Hound* Reporter!

As the Royal Bath & West Champion Exmoor we took part in a Cuddy Championship Qualifier with the other equine champions. Afterwards, we were directed into the collecting area where the show jumpers were busy warming up and it was lively. A reporter from *Horse & Hound* came up to interview me about Bear. Delighted to speak with her, but aware of Bear's Capriole, I suggested that we move to somewhere quieter to talk. But the reporter had a lot of people to interview, so we endeavoured to chat in the bustling warm up area. Suddenly, a show jumper cantered up behind us and Bear unleashed his Capriole. This had the show jumper rearing up and reeling backwards and Bear unfortunately also managed to take out the *H&H* reporter, who was knocked flat to the ground – and none too amused. I had a sinking feeling that our mention in *Horse & Hound* would be less than complimentary. Bear wrote a letter of apology to *H&H* pronto on our return home, but on reading the write-up on Royal Bath & West Show a couple of weeks later, I noted that the Champion Exmoor had behaved 'true to type', having been 'bought at a roadside sale'. Oh Dear.

Tempering Bear's Capriole by Dealing with my Own Insecurity!

I resolved to work on Bear's Capriole – and I received some sound advice from Classical stallion trainer Jenny Rolfe. She said that the problem could well be emanating from me.

'The stallion will look to protect you. If you are concerned and keep glancing behind you, the stallion will feel he has to deal with that 'threat'.' She told me to keep calm and confident, look ahead and keep his focus on me – and then it would most likely stop. She was right. Things got a lot better after that. Bear had simply been feeding off my worries that something or someone might come too close behind. When I stopped worrying about it, so did he. Although walking or riding into the backside of a stallion when he doesn't know you, is never a wise thing to do.

Bear is Mysteriously Difficult

At our next show, taking place at an equestrian centre, I asked my helper if she'd please stay with Bear at the trailer while I did the ridden class with Harry. She rolled her eyes and I sort of understood – you could be forgiven for thinking the crown jewels were in the trailer. Nevertheless, I felt it prudent to leave someone at the trailer with him at shows. As the ridden class came to an end, in which Harry did well, I noticed my helper watching from the gallery. I mouthed to her to 'go back to Bear!' She did. As I led Harry back to the trailer, she looked slightly panicky.

'Is he OK?'

She nodded, 'He seems to be.'

But he wasn't. When I'd left for the ridden class, Bear had been calmly munching his hay, not exactly happy at being left in his trailer but quiet. By now he was getting used to going to shows.

When I stopped worrying about what was behind us, Bear's Capriole stopped

Opposite page, top and middle: Bear standing Champion Exmoor at Royal Bath & West Show, 2007

Opposite, bottom: Champion Exmoor at the NPS Summer Championships 2007

However, as I led him out of the trailer, he was agitated and edgy and tried to nip me.

I knew I'd have my hands full – very full as it turned out. Bear was difficult to lead and not happy to have people approach him today. This included the judge and he bit her finger soundly as she waved them somewhat enticingly in front of his mouth while assessing him. She rushed off to get her finger bandaged while we all waited – and while I waited, excruciatingly embarrassed. Bear looked wide-eyed, like a belligerent teenager.

'That was very naughty Bear, I don't know what's come over you!' I whispered to him. Returning to the ring, the judge selected the final line-up, where Bear stood in second place.

She told him he was very lucky to be there, not waving her fingers in front of his mouth this time.

On returning home, we pondered the show and my helper wondered what had come over Bear.

'I wonder indeed,' I said. 'He behaved like he'd eaten a handful of caffeine tablets or something.'

NPS Summer Championships and the Exmoor Pony Breed Show

A trip to the prestigious NPS Summer Championships at Malvern saw Bear stand Champion Exmoor in the breed classes and Harry win the mares and geldings class. A week later, at the Exmoor Pony Annual Breed Show Bear stood Reserve Youngstock champion and Moorbred Champion.

Riding Bear On

That winter, I continued to ride Bear lightly to consolidate his acceptance of a rider. He has an exceptionally strong neck and at times he would decide he was going somewhere – such as helping himself to something in the hedgerows which can be better described as 'hedge-diving' – that wasn't part of my riding plans. Normal riding aids had literally no effect once Bear's determination was engaged and I did not want to be hard on his mouth and 'yank' him back on course. Or pull the bit through his mouth. As a stallion, he needed to understand not to do this – particularly if he decided to approach a mare he liked the look of when passing horses in the lanes, or out at a show. So I found the Fulmer bit, with its long cheek pieces, helpful for 'steering' in those early days of riding.

Chapter 6

Bear's First Mares and a Marriage

Bear's First Mare Arrives

Early in 2008, with Bear rising four, Otis was becoming increasingly uncomfortable at being the only companion of a maturing, testosterone-fuelled stallion.

It was time to start thinking about a suitable mare for Bear – and an escape route for poor Otis. A moorbred mare called Maisie (her official name is Hawkwell Smarty Pants) was suggested. Due to personal circumstances, Maisie's owner couldn't continue to look after her. She was a true 'old-fashioned, quality moorland type' of Exmoor pony and could well be an ideal brood mare for Bear, so I went to see her. I approached her carefully in the yard, letting her sniff my hand, then reached up to stroke her neck and towards her poll. She turned her head towards me and I stroked her nose. It was an instant and powerful connection. I moved away slightly and she stepped towards me.

'What a wonderful gentle mare,' I said.

Exmoors are curious – they choose their people and today, Maisie had chosen me. Her owner was delighted and relieved. There was no question that she would be joining me as Bear's first mare and the foundation mare for the new stud. It was too early in the season to introduce Maisie to Bear, however, Otis was now spending a lot of time standing at the field gate with an expression that implied, 'For goodness sake get me out of here!' It was very much time to make some changes as the rather mighty Bear was ready to cover mares. He could see Maisie from across the road sometimes and they called to each other. This all boded well for a few weeks time.

Planning Bear's First Mares

I received a call from the owner of a top level showing mare about bringing her to be covered by Bear, and this looked like it would be a very good pairing. However, the owner was keen to bring her mare in March, which meant I would have to introduce Maisie to Bear even earlier, if I wanted them to establish a good relationship before the visiting mare arrived. I wnted Maisie to be confident in her position as 'lead mare', as it was likely that there would be various visiting mares over the coming years and the plan was for them to run naturally with Bear.

Opposite page: Bear meets Maisie and spends his first season running with mares

Top and centre: Bear and Otis in their final days living together

Above: Otis spends much time sleeping after leaving Bear

Opposite: Bear with Maisie and at the 2008 Stallion Parade

Immense Relief for Otis

When I collected Otis from the field and brought him over to the yard to start introducing him to the horses and Harry, he walked into the manege and shortly afterwards, lay down and slept soundly. This happened often over the next few weeks. It was customary to see more of the large, beige underbelly of the otherwise almost black Otis than we saw of his face, as he snored and slept and recovered from the final months of keeping a young and rather frustrated stallion company.

Introducing Maisie to Bear

On taking Maisie over to Bear's field, there was a roar from Bear as he galloped down the field for the introduction. Maisie made a few attempts to kick him away, then decided he was actually rather gorgeous. From this very first covering Bear demonstrated that, rather than aggressively leaping onto mares and immediately covering them, as some young stallions are prone to do, he had a natural ability to seduce the mares. He showed Maisie his most impressive postures and then gently sniffed noses, licking her shoulder and winning her over. Within a few minutes of this, Maisie had come into full season and was covered. After this, Bear trotted across to me, with Maisie in tow, as if looking for approval. It was a special moment. Finally, my little Exmoor colt had become a full-blown stallion.

Not long afterwards, his first visiting mare arrived and her owner was pleased to see that she too was also treated with care by Bear. He had to work hard to win her over, but he did it with style and grace. He now had plenty to think about with two mature mares to manage – or be managed by – and his first little herd, which subsequently increased with the arrival of another top level mare.

Showing Bear as a Four-year-old Working Stallion at Devon County Show

Now running with his first mares, I nevertheless took Bear to the 2008 Exmoor Pony Stallion Parade and then to Devon County Show that May. It is fair to say that I did notice the difference. If someone had handed me this magnificent four-year-old stallion a few years previously and said, 'Go and show him,' I think I would have run a record-breaking mile in the opposite direction. But we'd been progressing together since he was a newly-weaned foal so it was less daunting. He stood second in a very strong class that day. I now had to learn how to successfully manage and show Bear as a fully working stallion.

Life Turns Upside Down – and a thunderbolt

A trip to the National Pony Association of Cornwall Summer Show (July 2008) saw Bear collect another Championship and things were going well. At around this time, I needed to source a new supplier of haylage and asking around, local farmer Nick Westcott was the name that kept coming up. Arranging for him to visit, I was on the yard with the ponies when I heard a vehicle parking outside the gate. I walked across to greet Nick and I can only describe it as a light being switched on all

around. He felt the same. It was a whirlwind for us both and only eight weeks after that we had the most wonderful wedding.

The day after meeting Nick, I took Bear to the South West Pony Association Summer show and he stood Champion Exmoor. He behaved very well and looked fantastic – his coat was gleaming and living with mares obviously suited him.

A Westcott Family History Involving Exmoor Ponies

Nick mentioned that his family had been involved in Exmoor ponies for many years and it transpired that his great grandfather, A G Westcott, was a founding committe member of the Exmoor Pony Society in 1921. He, along with his two brothers, had founded the original Exmoor pony herds 10, 11 and 21. The family had lived and farmed in the local parishes of Exmoor for over 500 years and in records we have found so far, mention of the Exmoors dates back to 1872. Nick's cousin, Malcolm Westcott, owns the free-living Westwilmer Herd 4 that runs on the Dunkery Commons today. Nick is a life-long horseman and it was clear he had an affinity and empathy with horses. Bear accepted Nick straight away – he was calm and relaxed around the stallion, which was reciprocated.

A New Life in the Porlock Vale of Exmoor

With our imminent wedding, my focus turned away from showing the ponies in the latter part of the season, and they got to enjoy quite a holiday. The move to Holt Ball was exciting and amazing and the horses and ponies were delighted with their beautiful new pastures. With the farm at only 400ft above sea level at the highest point and the Gulf Stream air flowing in and around Porlock Vale, there is a temperate climate where it is not uncommon to see the grass growing in February. There was an enormous range of moorland and vale out-riding.

However, plans to progress Bear's ridden work that winter were put on hold after a fall from one of my Arabians resulted in me breaking my collarbone – he'd caught his foot and tripped, pitching me into a bank. This required about eight weeks to heal which took us into the new year and Bear into his fifth year. 2009 would bring the arrival of Bear and Maisie's first foal, who we eagerly awaited.

So far, I'd only fallen off Bear once, but it had been a good reminder of who and what I was riding. I had done up the girth and got straight on. Bear must have been breathing in at the time and as he breathed out again, I hadn't given him time to adjust to the new tightness around his middle. This triggered an enormous buck. On reflection, just waiting those extra few seconds for him to breathe, adjust, take in what was happening and then get on would have been polite. I had been rather thoughtless and distracted. Bear launched high into the air, ejecting me onto the grass verge. When we stood together again, he looked somewhat aggrieved.

'I'm so sorry Bear,' I gasped. 'That was thoughtless of me.' We stood for a little while longer, mainly for my benefit as I was somewhat winded – and then I knew I had to get on again. I'll admit that my

Opposite page from top:
Bear Standing Champion
Exmoor NPA Cornwall
Summer Show;
Champion Exmoor at
SWPA Summer Show;
Nick and Dawn on their
wedding day

Left: Holt Ball Farm in the
National Trust Holnicote
Estate

Remembering to be mindful
on Bear's early rides

legs felt like jelly but off we went for our ride. It was a lesson in mindfulness. Take your time, stay focused and don't be cross with your pony if he dumps you. There is absolutely no point in that – it will only destroy trust.

That tendency to dramatically express his feelings was part of Bear's natural psyche and who he was as a result of his experiences. Having a creative temperament myself, I could empathise. We both needed to develop appropriate responses to things we didn't much like. Bear brought out an incredible capacity for patience in me – and despite the odd hiccup, I was starting to see that reciprocated in Bear.

Chapter 7

Bear's First Foals and Hot Branding Fury

Bear and Maisie's First Foal – and it's a Filly!

In March Maisie produced a beautiful filly foal, born secretly in the night as Exmoor mares tend to do, and Bear was there to see his daughter's arrival.

In the morning, however, he wasn't allowed anywhere near the foal and this continued for a few days, until Maisie decided it was suitable to allow him to introduce himself. We decided to name Bear's foals after volcanoes as his official name was Hawkwell Versuvius. A subterranean Caribbean volcano called Kick 'em Jenny was irresistible. So Jenny was named.

A Curious Hiccup before Devon County Show

With Devon County Show imminent in May, Bear was streamlined, fit and in show condition. He was looking great and fatherhood suited him. He had bonded with his filly foal Jenny and they adored each other. It was fascinating to see the interactive role that the stallion plays in helping to raise foals, when able to live in a family herd. However, a strange thing happened shortly before the show. I had left Bear, Maisie and Jenny in their paddock that evening. Early the following morning, Nick alerted me that they were not there and we went in search of them. We discovered them down the lane, curiously shut into some of the haylage fields. It was May and the grass was rich, young and lush. The ponies were having a wonderful time – and Bear's ample belly indicated that they had clearly been in

Bear and his first daughter, Holtball Kick 'em Jenny

Left: Bear's visiting mares

Opposite: Bear at the back with Holtball Kick 'em Jenny, then from left – Maisie, Monty and Monty's dam

there for most of the night. There was no way the effects of this would disappear by the following morning, where the Exmoors were to be shown at about 8am. Despite looking gleaming and glossy, he also looked like he'd been gorging himself on a large field of mowing grass. What timing. He came a respectable second in a large class, but the judge remarked, 'Watch his waistline.' Yes indeed. How unfortunate that his little foray to the haylage field had occurred so close to Devon County Show.

Visiting Mares Arriving and Royal Cornwall Show

This year, at five years old, Bear had a number of visiting mares and we moved them to a large, level pasture with good natural shelter. There was plenty of room for the new mares to meet Bear and each other. Jenny was the only foal until a visiting mare arrived with a tiny foal at foot offering the benefit of a much-needed playmate. There were great opportunities to observe herd behaviour and interactions as Bear attempted to bring some order to the situation. He was looking magnificent from all this work and when we took him Royal Cornwall Show, he stood Champion Exmoor once again. That evening when we returned him to the mares he roared and took off like a rocket across the field, leaving us wondering how on earth he'd managed to contain himself and behave so well at the show.

2009 Royal Cornwall Champion Exmoor

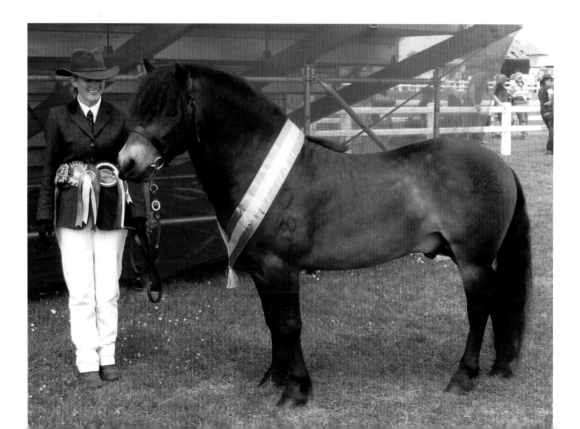

The Arrival of Bear's Son Monty

In June, I received news that a visiting mare from the previous year had produced a rather lovely colt foal – and I went to see him. The foal was indeed something special with a beautiful head and lovely proportions. Nevertheless, a filly had been much hoped for. We had recently purchased a mare from the colt's owner and subsequently realising she would rather have kept the mare, she asked if I would consider selling her back. It was agreed that the colt foal would be included as part exchange for the mare, and we would bring both him and his dam back to Holt Ball until weaning time. This meant she could be covered by Bear again – hopefully producing the desired filly the following year (which is what happened). It would also give us the opportunity to get to know the colt and Jenny would have a playmate again.

Naming Monty

The colt needed a name and as the intention was to run him on as a potential stallion, I was keen for him to be named after a volcano, like his father. However, his breeder wanted him to be named after a red wine, the theme she used for all her colts, with the fillies being named after white wines. She suggested Beaujolais. That was tricky. So I set to work researching volcano names in the vague hope of making a link. With some success as it turned out. In France, there is a dormant volcano named Mont de Brouilly, so with Brouilly a red wine in the Beaujolais family, we had the perfect solution. I could call the colt Monty for short. Fortunately his breeder agreed and so the colt foal was named Mont De Brouilly.

Bear recognised the mare and accepted Monty with no problem. There is a different dynamic with a stallion and colt foal, compared to a filly foal – the play is more robust and the colt endeavours to mirror his father's behaviours and body language. Both foals adored their father and spent hours with him, as well as playing with each other. He would take them off while the mares relaxed and grazed and it was clear that Bear loved his new role as a father.

Top: Monty as a foal

Above: Maisie and Jenny

NPA Cornwall Success and Obnoxious Behaviour at our Local Show

Bear stood Champion Exmoor and Overall M&M Champion Stallion at the Native Pony Association of Cornwall Summer Show. It was a fun day and a friendly show. However, we were about to experience a not so fun day at one of our local shows. This particular show is a long-standing Westcott family tradition and it would be the first time an Exmoor pony from our family's newly established Exmoor pony herd would be seen there. A substantial trophy was on offer to the Champion Exmoor. We were looking forward to an enjoyable day and a useful outing for young Bear. Unfortunately, we were loudly and unpleasantly heckled inside and outside of the ring. It was embarrassing for everyone, including the show organisers, who are always keen to attract quality exhibits. However the trophy spent the year at Holt Ball.

An Enlightening Trip to California to Study with Monty Roberts

In August, Nick and I spent a week at Flag Is Up Farms in California, attending Monty Roberts' special week long clinic. Each day, Monty gave tutorials and demos from morning until evening, and endeavoured to impart as much of his knowledge and philosophies as possible. Discussions with him continued through lunchtimes and we experienced the rehabilitation of some extremely wild and damaged horses, who had been brought to Monty as their last chance. This included a beautiful young Andalusian who had become petrified of being ridden after having his nose broken by the Seretta while being trained to rear for the Fiesta in Spain, and an abused Mustang mare who had learned to attack people. The over-riding message was that 'violence is never the answer'. We took a great deal away with us – particularly learning about Monty's fine-tuned and gentle advance and retreat approach to win the trust of wild deer – and we made some enduring friendships during the week. It was also a good opportunity to see Maya Horsey again, who was now running Monty's International Learning Centre.

The Re-establishment of Herd 11

As summer departed, we prepared our two foals, Monty and Jenny, for their inspection so they could be registered as pedigree Exmoor ponies. These were Bear's first progeny and we would need a herd number and prefix. In fact, this was now an historic family matter. Nick had been researching his ancestors involvement in Exmoor ponies and was interested to understand what had happened to the original herd numbers allocated to them. While Herd 10 had passed to another Westcott family (not related to Nick) and Herd 21 had been taken over by a breeder in Scotland, Herd 11 remained dormant. Records showed that it had been allocated to an unrelated lady who had bred one foal in the 1960s but none since. So Herd 11 appeared to be 'in limbo'. We contacted the Exmoor Pony Society and were told that we would need the permission of the herd owner to take over the herd number. Eventually, Nick got in contact with the family who were happy to bequeath Herd 11 back into the Westcott family and we chose the prefix 'Holtball'. So our first homebred Exmoor pony foal would be registered as Holtball Kick 'em Jenny 11/2. Although I had brought the Exmoor ponies to the marriage, it was my husband who provided the Herd number and prefix.

The Hot Branding Saga

Opposite page: Bear stood Champion Exmoor and Champion M&M Stallion at NPA Cornwall Summer Show which qualified him for the NPA Champion of Champions Final, pictured

As autumn arrived we arranged an inspection date with the breed society. All foals have to be microchipped for identification purposes and it had not occurred to us to hot brand our foals. They were not going to be running out on the moor and we both disliked the practice. Nick was by now fully aware of the personality quirks – both fearful and resentful – of the branded ponies and found the number of brands applied to the foals shoulders and rumps excessive – and barbaric. However, a spectacular row was about to erupt. A few weeks before our inspection was due to take place, Monty's

breeder mentioned that she would be relieved when she saw him branded (meaning that he had passed the inspection).

'Er, I think we're expected to have Monty hot branded,' I said to Nick.

'Don't be ridiculous Dawn, no one is going to brand our foals if we don't want them branded,' said Nick.

However, it was written in the Exmoor Pony Society Rules that the decision to brand lay with 'the breeder'. We were the owners of Monty but not the breeder.

'The breeder decides if the foal is branded,' came the response from the Exmoor Pony Society, when enquiring about this.

'But he's our foal and we don't want to hot brand him,' we said.

We were told that the branding irons would be brought to our inspection.

'Time for a good equine lawyer,' said Nick, getting on the phone.

To cut a long story short, a top equine lawyer confirmed in writing to the society that the foal was indeed our property (chattel) and no-one could do anything to our property unless we gave permission and that included hot branding him. It was also pointed out that the society's rule, which stated that the breeder decides about hot branding, would need to be changed in the event that the breeder was not the owner at the time of inspection. As we had become the owners of Monty prior to his inspection, an important legal point was clarified. Monty was not to be hot branded after all.

We had agreed to be a 'Foal Inspection Centre' and another owner had brought her foal to be inspected along with ours. She had requested that he be hot branded. As we didn't own him and hadn't bred him, we had no jurisdiction over the process. So the branding irons were indeed brought to our inspection, however, that would be the last time any hot branding of Exmoor pony foals took place at Holt Ball.

Monty is Abruptly Weaned and Says Goodbye to his Mother

After our own foals were inspected and passed, Monty's breeder arrived to take his dam away. Monty was only five months old and we would have liked to have kept them together for another month or two, but it was not possible. Monty went to his mother for a last suckle and, whether or not he knew it was the last time, he drank more frantically than he ever had before – and the milk ran out of his nose and onto the floor. The mare was led away, Monty looked after her and neither of them made a sound.

After Monty's mother left, and Maisie made it very clear that he was not going to suckle from her, Bear had a little shadow who remained glued to him. Monty must have taken great comfort from still having the familiar presence of his father, as well as Maisie and Jenny.

The Hot Branding of the Remaining Foal

The inspectors then turned their attention to the visiting foal who was in a separate stable. He was a super colt and we'd seen him in the show ring with his mother during the season. He passed his inspection and then the hair on his rump and shoulder area was clipped away. The branding irons were heated up and we watched as the inspectors applied the Exmoor pony star brand to his shoulder. The colt struggled, clearly feeling the searing burning as the iron was held in place.

The inspector agreed that the branding irons weren't hot enough, so they were heated up again and the sizzling red hot metal was re-applied onto the partially-burned area. Unsurprisingly, this time the colt foal reared up and tried to launch himself up and away from them.

Nick muttered an expletive as we watched.

'I think you'd better go and help hold him, for his own good, or he's going to do even more damage to himself,' I said, feeling queasy. There was nothing we could do to stop it. So Nick went to help for the sake of the foal.

The branding irons failed to be hot enough more than once, so the poor colt was really put through it with the applications of three different sets of branded marks on his shoulder and rump. Eventually it was over. The inspectors left and the foal's owner came in for tea. When I went back to the stable to check on him, the foal's eyes were glazed and hollow and he looked lost, like he was somewhere else – and in pain.

'You poor little chap. I'm really sorry that I couldn't do anything to stop this today. But this unnecessary practice will stop. I promise you that. It doesn't make it any better for you, but it will make it a lot better for a lot of foals after you. I will never forget what you've been through.'

In the place of the happy little chap was a typical multiple hot-branded Exmoor pony foal who would likely retain fear and anger-based, unpredictable responses thereafter. This was born out some time later, when his concerned new owner contacted me to ask if I had any idea why he was fearful and defensive when she tried to handle him on the nearside, while more tolerant on the offside. At least understanding what happened to him has enabled her to find the compassion and patience to nurture him through his fears.

Surely, it would be far better if the ponies were not subjected to unnecessary suffering in the first place? Especially when ponies born and living off the moor do not even require this kind of visual identification, involving third degree burns and unsightly life-long scars. Nick and I certainly felt so – and we were not alone.

Monty's last day with his mother

Opposite page: Bear and his 2009 foals Monty and Jenny

Chapter 8

Horse Agility and Showing Success

Discovering Agility for Ponies

Early in 2010 I discovered that a new equestrian activity was emerging in the form of agility for horses.

Although the concept had been around for some years, with impressive YouTube videos, particularly of one amazing horse and handler completing an agility obstacle course at liberty in Finland (Hevosagility: Reading ref: 2009 'Horse Agility – Liberty Horse Training' by Koikka Loikka) – it had not yet taken off in the UK. Fortunately for us, a Devon-based horse trainer was encouraging people to try horse agility taster sessions followed by a mini-competition. She was relaxed about me bringing along a stallion and was an Exmoor pony owner herself. At the clinic, there would be other horses and ponies in the arena with us, as well as all kinds of new obstacles and challenges. I was excited and intrigued – this could be just what we were looking for to progress our understanding and Bear's confidence. Everything would take place in head collars with long (10ft or 12ft ropes). It sounded brilliant.

Bear Shows an Early Aptitude for Horse Agility

Introducing equines to new obstacles and tasks like a flapping plastic curtain, a bridge, a tunnel, a big plastic hoop, hula hoops, a rope gate, umbrellas, carrying filled sacks on their backs, tarpaulin, narrow gaps and brightly coloured balls, etc, while in an arena with half a dozen others doing the same, on a windy day, in a strange place – seemed like a challenge for sure. Bear surpassed my expectations, showing an aptitude for learning new tasks and he won the mini-competition in the afternoon. This fascinating day had strengthened our partnership, enabled us to face the unexpected and above all – it had been fun, interesting and educational. I was hooked. This was what I'd been looking for.

Above and opposite:
Bear showed great interest in and aptitude for Horse Agility. Pictured here at an agility event

The idea was to create a competition league where horses and ponies from across the world could compete. This was all evolving while I continued to show and ride Bear that year and I looked forward to becoming involved.

The Arrival of Elbrus

Maisie's second foal, a handsome colt who we named after the Russian mountain and volcano Elbrus, arrived in March. Once again, Bear was with Maisie to witness his birth and this time, he was allowed to say hello a little earlier as Maisie was more relaxed with her second foal. Monty and Jenny had now been introduced to 'Uncle' Harry and Otis, our trusted geldings, who proved to be wonderful babysitters, who provided them with much-needed company and guidance after separating from Maisie and Bear.

Was Multiple Hot Branding Illegal After All?

During the winter we'd been taking a close look at the hot branding situation. Although the practice was still permitted in England and Wales, under the The Mutilations (Permitted Procedures) (England) Regulations 2007 that accompanied the Animal Welfare Act 2006, it stipulated that 'unnecessary suffering' must not be caused to an animal. Therefore, where there were an excessive number of hot branded marks applied to multiple sites on the foals bodies, or where the practice was carried out on foals that did not need 'visual ID' in addition to a microchip – this would surely constitute 'unnecessary suffering'? Despite pointing this out, it was clear that there was going to be considerable resistance to stopping Multiple Hot Branding – and ceasing all hot branding of tame Exmoor foals born off the moor.

Bear's Visiting Mares and Royal Bath & West Show 2010

At six years old, Bear found himself running with a significant herd comprising our own and visiting mares. Holtball Elbrus was the only foal and spent much of the day watching and imitating his father and developing immense presence along the way. I was keen to maintain a good connection with Bear and brought him up to the farm to ride and work with on a regular basis. On the way back through the fields and tracks to his mares, I'd turn him loose and this was the emergence of a true liberty connection. There was a special moment one day, when I opened the gate into his field and he began to trot off towards the mares. Then he stopped and came back to me, as if acknowledging our connection. He once again started to move off and after pausing to mark the ground, galloped flat out to the mares. He had been so polite and thoughtful. Watching his immense power, I was amazed how he managed to retain such gentleness with me.

Unfortunately, running with a considerable herd meant that Bear bore the marks of his feisty mares which included a robust hoof print on his chest and a few other grazes. It wasn't exactly the ideal presentation for the perfect show pony. However, he was also fully fit, muscled up, full of presence and gleaming with health. When the judge at Royal Bath & West Show examined him and saw the hoof print, I apologised and said, 'I'm sorry about this, he's come from the mares this morning.' The judge smiled and said it was exactly what he'd expect an Exmoor stallion to be doing

Above and opposite, bottom left: Bear with Maisie and Holtball Elbrus

Opposite, bottom right: Maisie protects Holtball Elbrus from action between Bear and the visiting mares

and Bear was awarded the championship despite the battle scars. He was also called out in the final six of the Cuddy championship qualifier and there was no hint of a Capriole. It was a good day.

In July we took Bear to an NPS Area show, where he stood Mountain and Moorland In Hand Champion. He had a powerful energy and I was well aware that we needed to channel it somewhere. Agility may well be the answer but the competition format and structure was not yet up and running.

Bear's First Ridden Class at a Local Show

We decided to take Bear back to our local show, this time as a novice ridden pony rather than to the in hand class. It was his first time out at a show under saddle and he could be described as 'green'. As it wasn't far, I hacked over to the show to warm him in. We shared the ring with lead rein children and all sorts of native ponies in the Mountain and Moorland class. The judge, a familiar face this time accompanied by a probationary judge, curiously decided to take hold of Bear's mouth with both hands and look at his teeth, and also pick up and examine his front foot – while I was mounted and in the line-up. Physical handling of exhibits by judges in such classes is unorthodox and could well have provoked a dangerous explosion from a novice ridden, moorbred Exmoor stallion. Bear's ears lay flat and sideways – not a good sign. He tensed like a coiled spring and turned his head slightly to stare back at me. I breathed calmly and without taking my hands off the reins, gently stroked his wither. He held and produced a reasonable novice ridden show and we were placed fourth. I was proud of him for coping with the experience. He put in a leap on the way out of the ring and under the circumstances I could understand why. I felt rather similar myself.

Above: Royal Bath & West Show Champion Exmoor 2010

Left: The judge taking hold of Bear's face during the M&M ridden class

Opposite: Bear spent much time with his colt foal Holtball Elbrus

Success at the Exmoor Pony Breed Show

A couple of weeks later we took Bear to the Exmoor Pony Breed Show and were thrilled to see him once again stand Overall Supreme In Hand Champion. This time, competing for the Supreme of Show was Bear, along with the Ridden Champion, a gelding called Tawbitts Mystic Major. The judges awarded it to the ridden gelding and the shriek of delight from one of his owners, Mrs

Hawkwell Versuvius 'Bear' – Overall Supreme In Hand Champion and Reserve Supreme Champion of the Exmoor Pony Breed Show 2010

Hilary Williams, was heartfelt. It was wonderful that Bear had claimed the Supreme In Hand crown once again and stood Res Supreme of Show – and Tawbitts Mystic Major went on to compete a number of times at both HOYS and Olympia. This time, our trophies included an historic one which was mounted on various plated stands that depicted all of the adult In Hand Champions since the breed show began.

A Surprise Physical Attack

While we were thrilled with Bear's success, at a local party I was 'playfully attacked' with a powerful toy water gun. My assailants left the party soon afterwards, but it had put somewhat of a dampener on the evening.

The attack had a profound effect on me. While being restrained against my will, I had felt violated. It made me think about how newly weaned foals, used to living wild and free in the safety and familiarity of their family herd, must feel during the process of being physically grabbed, restrained and Multiple Hot Branded as their first contact with humans. The experience strengthened my resolve to campaign for welfare improvements for Exmoor ponies. Monty Roberts quote once again sprung to mind, 'Violence is never the answer'.

Onwards and Upwards and a Return to Horse Agility

In late 2010, it was announced that an international agility competition league would start in January and continue through the year with an overall winner announced in December. Competitors from around the world would complete the same courses and then film and submit entries, to be judged by the central team. The idea was to accumulate points and work up through the levels, from Starter to Advanced. With a useful barn area and plenty of scope for making and sourcing the obstacles, we decided to give it a go. There would be monthly classes 'on the line' and also some liberty classes, where the ponies would compete loose.

It sounded like enormous fun and would require a whole new level of understanding between Bear and myself – and help his confidence and development. The sport was a particularly exciting concept for small breed native ponies like Exmoors, who are intelligent, curious, independent-thinking and excellent at problem solving – they meet many obstacles and challenges out on the moor. Often, people may be too large or don't want to ride them, so agility looked like an interesting and fun 'job' for them within the equestrian world. I felt that if Bear and I could become good at agility, it would be a wonderful way to showcase the attributes of the Exmoor pony.

After an unwelcome physical attack in the autumn of 2010, the announcement of a new horse agility competition gave us something positive to look forward to. Pictured: Alyson Govier on Hawkwell Honey Buzzard and Dawn on Bear

Chapter 9

Secrets of Success with Liberty and Agility

Preparing for Agility

To successfully compete at agility, the horse must be supple and flexible.

He must be responsive to moving his feet without resistance; sending away and drawing back to the handler; able to bend his body and generally allow the direction of his movements to navigate various challenges and obstacles safely and smoothly. This requires going over, through, under and around various objects – and also moving forwards, backwards, sideways and circling – often with precision and always with willing participation. There has to be understanding and acceptance from both horse and handler and there is an emphasis on 'good horsemanship', rather than force and coercion. No whips, shouting or other negative influences are allowed.

Connection – When you Turn your Horse Loose, all you are Left with is The Truth

Establishing a genuine Positive Connection between horse and handler is essential for horse agility. Mutual trust and understanding are core to achieving this. Given the choice, a horse will not stay with anyone he does not want to be with. When you turn a horse loose, you are left with The Truth. Does he want to be with you or not? To get a horse to stay with you and carry out a series of tasks, the horse has to want to do what you are asking. Seeing him walk or trot away because, given the choice, he would prefer to be somewhere else, can be a blow to the human ego. It's easy to convince yourself that your horse loves you, when he's standing there, held by a head collar and lead rope. Turning loose shows you where your relationship with your horse is really at. In order to succeed at liberty and agility, you have to face who you really are – because that is who your horse sees and responds to.

Opposite: Bear navigating the see-saw

It takes enormous courage for a horse to 'let you in'

Below: When you turn a horse losoe, you are left with the truth

Authenticity and Courage

Building a successful horse/human relationship for agility therefore requires a willingness to be authentic. For a lot of people – including myself – this takes a degree of self development and personal adjustment – and honesty.

For the horse, it takes enormous **courage** to allow a human into his heart and mind, and to reveal that he does indeed understand you, and is making the conscious choice to engage in the activities requested. Because through taking part, the horse reveals himself. Concealing and therefore protecting these aspects of his true self from humans is very much part of the horse's survival instinct.

So despite knowing each other well, Bear and I both still had an enormous amount of personal development to do – and trust to build – in order to progress at horse agility. I was asking a wild-born Exmoor stallion to open up his heart and mind to me – and work as a willing partner, at times loose and free of restraint.

There were some lessons to be learned and some truths to be faced if I wanted to be good at this exciting new equestrian sport.

Learning to be aware and mindful

The First Lesson – How Gentle is Your Horse Handling - Really?

I realised that I was, at times, more thoughtless in my approach with Bear than I would care to admit. By 'thoughtless' I don't mean that I was unkind to Bear. However, when I analysed my body language and requests, I realised that I could actually be quite abrupt and bossy. For example, on approaching Bear, I inevitably put the head collar straight over his nose and did it up. I wasn't being mindful in offering him the head collar, letting him process my intention and waiting for him to turn his head towards me, inviting him to put his nose into it. All of these subtle interactions offer the opportunity to read how the horse feels that day, and enables him to adjust to the fact you now want to 'control' his movements. I was missing all this because I just put the head collar straight on.

I was quite good at inviting him to come with me but, if there was some resistance, it was routine to tug on the rope and say, 'Come on Bear.' I wasn't inviting him to make the willing decision to move with me – with a smile in the line. I was missing these subtle nuances too.

When I led Bear from the nearside (the left) and I wanted to turn to the right, I'd lift my hand with the lead rope in it and wave it to manoeuvre him to the right. Not touching his face, but still in a 'we are moving that way Bear' manner. He might bump into me with his shoulder and if both he and I were feeling determined, there was plenty of scope for both of us to be a lot softer with our body language.

I was not being 'mindful' in the way you need to be with a horse if you want a true partnership. If we were going to be successful at horse agility, I would need to progress to a whole new level of gentle communication and understanding in our interactions. Or Bear would simply, when given the choice at liberty, leave me.

This awareness was exactly what Bear – and our partnership – had been waiting for. I was ready to learn – and the teacher who appeared was Bear himself.

The Second Lesson – How Connected are you to Your Horse's Feet and Core Energy?

When it came to learning agility, I realised that there was a world of communication in moving a horse's feet and making a connection that I needed to tune into. Of course, I understood the fundamental necessities in getting horses to move backwards, sideways, around, and come forwards – without resistance. But I needed greater awareness of the significance of each individual step.

When I asked Bear to move his quarters, it was easy to 'waggle' the end of the lead rope at him and 'make' him move, rather than thinking about how I conveyed my intention and made my requests – and where and how I directed my energy to achieve a calm, willing step.

Something else was missing. When I made a request, I wasn't consciously radiating my intention to Bear from my Core Energy Centre - the heart and solar plexus areas. I was effectively just making requests from 'inside my head' and backing them up with physical gestures. If necessary, I could 'use my energy' but again, I was missing the subtleties. Some trainers describe the use of energy as 'turning up a bunsen burner'. I realised that it was more like dealing with a soft radiating light – a silver or gold thread that connects human to horse. It is about communication – not force. Bear and I could vastly improve our communication if I could learn more about conscious energy connection.

Bear must have felt, at times, like he was dealing with a brick wall, when he faced a human trying to communicate through mechanical actions and speech, while fairly oblivious to the profound and powerful world of core energy connection. Horses engage in this all the time with each other – just think how quickly a herd can activate a collective flight response in unison. While humans rely heavily on speech to communicate – often backing that up with aggressive and ego-motivated actions when they feel they are not being listened to – and missing the nuances in between. I wanted to catch up fast.

Learning how to motivate a horse to move calmly and willingly, one step at a time, without resistance or 'scatting' away in alarm – and radiating and receiving energy between you and the horse – are key elements of liberty horsemanship communication.

The Third Lesson – How Mindful and Aware of Your Ego are You?

In order to recognise that we have a lot to learn, we have to deal with our egos. The ego can be powerfully obstructive and destructive if allowed to dominate. However, it can also be helpful in enabling you to progress – if managed appropriately. In its raw form, the ego can wail like a petulant child and cause you not to attempt things at which you may fail. It can also make you judgemental and scornful of learning. Recognising and quietening the ego, when venturing outside of your comfort zone, is essential in learning new skills – where humility, authenticity and mindfulness are needed to progress understanding.

My own ego needed managing in order for me to recognise and accept my ignorance and really open my mind to learning – on what appeared to be a very basic level but was nothing of the kind.

Managing The ego is essential in good horse training

The Fourth Lesson – Are you Grounded and In The Present Moment?

In horse training, the intelligent, analytical human mind can be both a blessing and a curse. We spend much time reasoning and rationalising everything 'in our heads' and sometimes forget to stand in the present moment and just 'feel it'. Creating a balance between what we are thinking and what we are feeling and seeing is vital in achieving good communication. We need to tune into what is *actually* happening, rather than what we *'think'* is happening.

Let's Take a Look at What this is Like for a Horse...

Imagine what it feels like for a horse standing there in front of a person who is busy thinking about what he wants to achieve, while his own ego is busy judging the situation and warning him not to make a fool of himself. At this point, the person is not really listening to his intuitive gut feelings, or

Being in the present moment and connecting with mindfulness is vital in building trust with horses

tuning into the present moment, or processing how the horse is feeling. He is not making an 'energy connection' with the horse and instead remains flat and disconnected in his solar plexus and heart centre.

Suddenly, the person activates the rope and conveys an abrupt physical instruction to the horse. As this has come out of the blue, the horse is startled and confused.

'What on earth do you want me to do?' the horse asks. 'What is your intention?'

The human is flustered that the horse hasn't responded and applies more pressure, his ego affronted that the horse has not obeyed him. The horse is alarmed (or annoyed) as the request wasn't clear in the first place and he either spooks away or stands there, uncertain. The handler gets annoyed and a punishment is administered to the disobedient and 'difficult' horse. The handler eventually gets a nip or a kick, or the horse pulls away – and so it goes on. This is an ignorant and brutal way of communicating with a horse – when you are not using your core energy and mindfulness to 'connect' before making a request. If we're honest, most of us have been there in one degree or another.

The Fifth Lesson – How Patient are You?

Learning what is required to successfully communicate with a horse as a willing partner – when we allow horses to be at liberty – requires patience. You cannot simply 'demand' that the horse does something. Because if he's loose, he can leave you. It is all about creating the right environment and understanding, reading how the horse feels, conveying your intention and requests clearly and appropriately, and achieving the required willing responses from the horse. Patience is truly a virtue. We have to learn about Horse Time.

Admitting that – in horse terms – I was actually quite impatient, missing myriad communications and fairly clumsy and unclear in my interactions with Bear as we started agility training, certainly had my ego wailing – and a good job too!

Above left: Bear navigating the S-Bend at liberty

Above right: Bear standing in the hula hoop while Dawn walks circles around him

Starting Horse Agility

At the 'starter' level of Horse Agility, I had to demonstrate that Bear could complete simple and straightforward tasks on a rope. These involved things like asking him to walk backwards through two poles; through a narrow space between drums; navigate a cone weave at walk; go under and through a curtain made from plastic ribbons; show he could walk, trot and halt as requested; walk over a brightly-coloured tarpaulin; move his quarters as requested; navigate through an L-Bend or S-bend; jump a small jump safely, etc. There were many different tasks and obstacles. Each month, a selection were chosen, which had to be completed in a specific order. We had to film the course with no editing and without the pony or handler leaving the camera frame. So this required not only being able to build and complete the course, but having a camera person film the entry within the rules – and the technical skills to process the entry. The video was then submitted and judged. Despite the geographical distance – this allowed us to compete with horses and ponies from across the globe.

Taking Care not to 'Drill' or Over-practice

While it's necessary to thoroughly learn the various tasks and obstacles, it's completely counterproductive to 'drill' tasks, over-practice or repeat the courses too many times. To get the best out of agility ponies, they need to remain 'fresh' and interested. Repeating the same sequence of tasks too many times while trying to get a 'perfect' entry can dull and even frustrate a pony. It is really important to get the balance of training right – and keep it fun.

The Core Connection Warm-up Exercises

Perfect for Liberty, Agility and Ridden Work

Liberty and horse agility involves being able to communicate with and engage the pony's mind and body to successfully complete a course. Bear and I needed a training plan.

With a wealth of horsemanship methods, philosophies and approaches to groundwork and liberty, I studied as much as I could – drawing on my existing knowledge, listening to advice, tips and ideas from a range of liberty trainers and horse people, including the agility competition team. Bear and I began to evolve a training routine that helped us to make a good connection, tune into and understand each other. The resulting **Core Connection Warm-up Exercises** opened an entire world of

communication for us – for both agility and liberty work, and also for riding.

With these straightforward **Core Connection Warm-Up Exercises**, the pony can reveal any anxiety and insecurities, blockages, resistance, stiffness, distractions, emotions, etc, and you can gently work through them, calming any worries and bringing focus and harmony to your working relationship. It's about 'getting into a good place' and tuning into each other. They can help to improve any horse/human partnership.

Equipment for the Warm-up Exercises

1) A head collar or halter;

2) A good quality long lead rope (preferably 12ft). A marine doublebraid rope can vibrate if you gently tap on it, which travels up to reach the horse under his muzzle – offering myriad opportunities for subtle communication, such as 'please stop now', 'please go back', or 'I'm about to ask you to do something'. Flat lines or conventional plaited lead ropes don't offer this sensitive 'feel'.

3) When the Warm-up Exercises are well established, you can do them at liberty, without a head collar/halter or rope.

Preliminary Exercises

Hand to Muzzle Greeting

When I greet a horse or pony out in the field or barn, the first thing I do is offer my hand, palm down, fingers relaxed, in a gentle greeting. I wait for the pony to choose to connect with me. Sometimes they will bump their muzzle onto my hand in greeting. Responses including sniffing at my hand and inviting me to turn my palm up so they can sniff or lick it – willingly

Bear's hand to Muzzle greeting at a demo

Putting on the head collar gently

connecting and exchanging energy. Or they may only want to touch my hand lightly with the palm remaining down. At other times, they might pause and choose not to touch my hand at all. Occasionally, if feeling unsure or out of sorts, they can even make a face at it, flicking their ears back or turning their head away. This is their choice and this simple greeting enables you to read a huge amount about the pony's frame of mind and attitude – and even health and wellbeing – that particular day.

Putting on the Head Collar or Halter
Rather than putting the head collar straight onto the nose, gently offer it, perhaps drawing it slightly away again, and see how accepting the horse is to have it put on. Much can be read from the horse's responses – does he tense, turn his face away, brace in the neck and poll area, remain stock still – or even move away? We're looking for the horse to acknowledge the head collar without tension and willingly accept it. Being mindful about the way you put on the head collar can convey a lot to the horse about your state of mind, attitude, mood and intention. Being quiet, gentle, kind, reassuring and respectful of his head and the fact he is giving up his freedom to you, is very helpful in motivating the horse to be your willing partner. When the head collar is on, pause. Let the horse adjust. When I started behaving like this with Bear, he often gave a relieved sigh. He found my new-found mindfulness reassuring.

Letting Outside Stress Go and Being In The Present Moment
Being mindful and in the present moment with the way you approach, greet and start interactions with your horse allows you both time to adjust – and importantly – the opportunity to let go of any distracting thoughts. Let it all go.

Remember to Repeat the Exercises Equally on Both Sides
Repeat each exercise on both sides of the horse to ensure there is balance. You may find that the horse finds one side easier than the other. This is neither right nor wrong – it's just something to note. Over time, as suppleness and understanding increases, the horse becomes more evenly balanced and confident. These gentle exercises are also an excellent way of identifying any stiffness and even injuries that may need further attention.

The Power of the Pause

After each of these warm up exercises, remember to relax and pause and ensure that the horse knows he has done the right thing. This enables you both to appreciate a place of peaceful 'core calmness' before the next exercise. Horses enjoy pauses and it also allows them time to process what they're doing, as well as reading that the handler's energy levels are remaining calm. They are constantly assessing if a situation is safe. Positive pauses give immense reassurance and an opportunity to consolidate learning.

Breathing

Through all these exercises it's important for the handler to breathe calmly and deeply, conveying that there is no tension, frustration or impatience and that all is good. This conveys a feeling of warmth, trust and safety to the horse.

Feeding Hand Treats

Broadly speaking, I don't like feeding multiple treats during a training session. I prefer to offer a food reward at the end of the session, from a bowl or on the ground, rather than from my hand. Working with stallions and also groups of ponies, I've found that repeated treating can get in the way of the connection – and particularly when I'm surrounded by a lot of ponies, it can encourage undesirable behaviour as they compete for food. What I'm striving to achieve is a pure energy connection and mutual understanding without the complication of food. Having said that, there are exceptions to every rule and every pony is different. Sometimes, feeding treats at key stages of the session works very well and adds value for the pony. Bear is one example and I sometimes use treats with him. So my rule of thumb is that if you feel the pony has done something that compels you to offer a treat, which enhances their understanding and experience – then do it. It's all about what feels right for you and the pony. If it feels right, it more than likely is right.

Remember to Smile – or at Least Have a Pleasant Expression

Horses can read and interpret facial expressions. It is therefore important not to frown or scowl, even in concentration. Imagine you are looking in a mirror – what kind of expression would you like to see reflected back at you, and consider what you are conveying to your horse with your face. Also remember to read your horse's facial expressions – they are capable of a lot more expressions than originally thought!

Remember to read facial expressions!

Exercise One - Moving (Yielding/Disengaging) the Quarters

With this exercise, there is no stick involved to motivate the horse to move the quarters. There is a distinct difference between making a horse move his quarters and achieving one willing step. First, we need to understand what the horse is conveying through the *way* he moves his quarters.

If a horse wants to retain his option to run away, he remains straight. Like a runner off a starting block. Think of the horse's hind quarters like your hips and legs. If you're feeling like you may need to run away fast from something, you balance and become poised, one leg positioned just behind the other, ready for you to launch away. The very last thing you do is stand with your legs crossed and your hips 'disengaged'. Just try it.

It's the same for a horse. If he is unsure and thinks he may want to leave the situation, and you ask him to move his quarters, he may say 'OK but I'm remaining straight, and will step his nearside leg away and behind him. At any time, from this position he can run away. The horse is saying, 'I'm moving my quarters but I don't trust you or the situation, so I'm remaining straight.'

We're looking for the horse to step his nearside hind leg 'through' – to cross his legs and disengage his quarters. From this position he is 'bending and yielding' – he can't easily run away. The horse has to feel safe enough to yield and bend. This is why one step at a time in this exercise is worth a thousand 'impressive' circles with a horse spinning or 'scatting' around you.

If there is resistance and your horse won't step anywhere, the very last thing he needs is a smack with the rope or a whack/tap with a whip, as all you are doing is using force and coercion to 'move your horse's feet.' Yes, you can make him do it, but you're not building trust or establishing two-way communication. You are just dominating your horse.

Look to Yourself

If a horse doesn't want to move, we need to look to ourselves.

Being spatially aware

Where am I asking him to move from? Am I inside his 'zone of pressure'? This pressure zone radiates immediately around a horse's body and here, his natural instinct is to move towards a predator and 'into pressure'. This stems from old times where horses were chased and hunted for food. At the point a predator reached the horse to sink in its teeth, the horse's natural instinct was to stop and move back into the attack, to lessen the tearing of flesh and to fight to disable the predator if possible. With these primal instincts, if we ask a horse to move away from us while too close, the horse is more likely to stand there or shift towards us.

This is all about spatial awareness and something we can be quite unaware of. Simply stepping away, outside of the pressure zone, and asking again can result in a dramatically different response. As trust builds, horses learn to move away from pressure willingly and calmly.

Another reason a horse may not move can be due to him placing 'resistance' in one or some of his feet and 'rooting' to the spot. If you look closely, you can usually see which foot seems particularly 'stuck'. Here, any anxiety, uncertainty, disinclination to do what you ask, etc, manifests itself. It is the feet that move the horse – and by rooting one or more of them, the horse is basically saying 'No, I don't want to.'

Of course, you can make someone do something by saying 'You will do this!' Often with horses, this 'No' is followed by a sharp smack or other admonishment from a handler. However, the 'No' can also mean, 'I'm not sure', or 'I'm not convinced this is safe,' etc. It is not simply 'disobedience'. So gently releasing resistance is an opportunity for the handler to communicate that what he's asking the horse to do is OK and safe. Through this two-way communication, we can negotiate with and reassure the horse – and motivate him to want to do as we ask – rather than force him.

So when faced with a horse that doesn't want to move, first ensure you are in a good position to make the request, outside of his pressure zone (which may be a few feet away), then radiate a clear intention and a beam of positive energy from your heart centre and solar plexus area. Literally 'feel' to the horse that you would like him to move his quarters, conveying a warm, trusting energy and feeling of safety. It's amazing how, when the handler makes an effort to convey this clearly, horses connect with it and respond positively by making a willing step.

When the horse takes that first step through with the hind quarters, pause and let him process it – and then repeat it a couple of times. Repeat the exercise on the other side. There's no need to keep asking for steps – once the request has been made and the horse has responded nicely – the job is done.

Exercise Two – Drawing the Head and Neck
Stand at the pony's shoulder and ask him to draw his head around to you. Depending on the pony's conformation, suppleness, stage of development and mood, this can range from a slight gesture to a full bend. This may be immediate and supple, or it can take a while if the pony is, for whatever reason, holding any tension in his neck – or distracted, insecure, resistant,

Drawing the head and neck to you

annoyed for whatever reason. This can be affected by the environment, noise, the weather, how the pony is feeling that day – and also the energy and intention he is reading in you. The important thing to achieve is a willing gesture – a willing 'try'. This is also a great way to test your patience, because if you're agitated to get on with whatever you want to do, distracted by outside thoughts or in any way not calm, peaceful and in the present moment – you will be rumbled here! Horses are highly sensitive to any inappropriate energy when you are standing by their neck and they will not want to turn their head into it. Reward what your horse offers you with a pause of appreciation.

Exercise Three – Sending (Yielding) the Head and Neck
The opposite exercise to drawing the head around to you is to ask the horse to bend (yield) his head and neck away from you. This should be requested without actually touching the horse's face, and should be a gentle and trusting yield away. The top of the horse's neck is a vulnerable area which he can remain

Sending (yielding) the head and neck away

Asking for a yielding whole body bend

protective about exposing. So if he is happy to yield his head and neck away from you, revealing that area, then trust is building between you. A 'send away' like this can be achieved by very gentle waving of the fingers up and adjacent to the horse's eye area – in a non-invasive and non-confrontational way that just says, 'please move away from me a little.' You are looking for a gentle yield away and one step away to the side, out from the shoulder – so the horse bends a little at the same time. A 'smile' should remain in the lead rope. Insecure horses may step forwards or backwards 'staying straight'. A step to the side demonstrates willingness to bend. Again, feel the intention of the request and radiate this positively to the horse through your hand as a clear request, rather than an 'order'.

Tip: Once this exercise is well-established, it brings finesse to the show ring performance as the pony understands how to bend and 'yield away' as you go around the ring – rather than trying to cross in front of you. These drawing and sending exercises also bring benefits to ridden work, as a light pressure or tap on the wither/base of neck conveys to the horse that you'd like him to turn or bend to the left or the right.

Exercise Four – Drawing the Head and Moving the Quarters – a Yielding Bend

Ask the horse to draw his head towards you, then gently touch the girth area and ask him to also yield his hind quarters away, stepping through. The head comes around, the quarters yield around and you are experiencing a whole, willing bend from the horse. By placing your hand lightly in the girth area to achieve this, you replicate the leg aid to yield. This exercise trains for a willing halt when ridden. This is your ultimate safety communication when riding tackless. A horse that doesn't want to bend and who wants to stay straight, is a horse that may well not stop when out riding, if motivated to take flight. It's the same when leading – a horse that won't bend is more likely to tank off when leading, if provoked. Horse and handler need this willing and understanding communication to stay safe. Remember to repeat on the other side – and pause to reward.

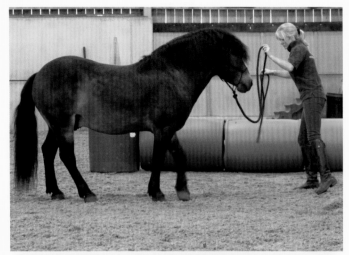

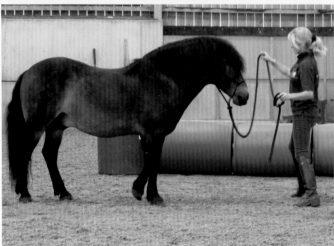

Asking the pony to open his shoulders and take one step to the side

Exercise Five – Opening the Shoulders

This exercise needs to be done with particular care, mindfulness and gentleness – because you are asking the horse to open his shoulders and therefore, his chest and heart centre, for you. Stand in front of the horse and make sure he is comfortable with you there. Open your arm and lift the rope away a little to the left, while starting to make one small step sideways to the left, inviting the horse to do the same. He may not understand at first, but will soon get the idea and will start to mirror the movement. If a horse is not used to this kind of suppling exercise, he may be tight in his pectorals, shoulder and neck muscles – and more so on one side than the other. If this is the case, gentle massaging in these areas can help. You're looking for one small step to the side from the horse. This is a wonderful exercise for opening and freeing up the shoulder, removing and unblocking tensions and suppling the horse for lateral work – either in agility or ridden. It is also a big trust-builder between you both.

This is an exercise to try when you feel comfortable with a horse and I'd advise taking particular care if you feel you are dealing with a defensive or aggressive horse to avoid a situation when they may think about lunging at you, particularly if they are stiff or sore in their muscles. When I worked with Bear on this exercise, it was clear that he found it a big ask. He was stiffer on one side than the other, and at first, he was insecure about taking a step sideways. This, more than any other of the exercises, requires the horse to admit that he clearly understands you and is able to 'mirror' your movements. Once Bear was confident of the exercise, he became very proud of it and now does it with gusto. So at the beginning, even a tiny lean in the right direction should be rewarded. Again, after each positive step, I pause and let the pony process what we've achieved.

Exercise Six – Backing Up

Ask the horse to take a step backwards by gently lifting the rope to convey your intention and tapping gently on it to send a small vibration. It is a request and not an order. 'I'm asking you to please step back.' It is important to feel this intention through your core energy centre (heart and solar plexus) and radiate a feeling that you would like the horse to step back. Horses can find this difficult for a variety of reasons. Not routinely being asked to move backwards from a handler, a horse can retain this direction as 'his own'. You are also asking them to move

backwards where they can't easily see. There may be danger back there. It's also quite predatory to stand in front of a horse and say 'Go Back!' which can be alarming for them. Depending on how they react to stress, they may scat away, or they may 'root' through planting that uncertainty into a hoof.

If the horse doesn't move, it is counter-productive to rapidly 'increase the pressure'. People routinely do this by using force and coercion to achieve the backwards step, such as flapping, violently rippling and snapping the rope, poking the horse in the chest, or using 'loud' body language. Any insecurities or resistance the horse may be harbouring will only be reaffirmed with this aggressive behaviour from the handler. It is better to work away quietly at achieving *one willing backward step*, than being hung up on making him go backwards with what you perceive is 'necessary pressure' to 'obey' your command. That is just your ego shouting.

One of the best ways to get a stuck horse to move backwards is to quietly step out to the side and look to each of his feet, seeing if you can gently 'unstick' each one and identify the foot that is 'planted'. Then return to standing in front of the horse and, ensuring you are not too close into the pressure zone, ask for a backward step again.

The horse will be trying to express how he feels and forcing backwards steps at this point misses the point. When one willing step is achieved, pause to reward and then ask for another step. If it's been difficult to achieve, you may want to end the exercise there on a good note. If it's been easy, you can request a few more steps backwards, again using the same gentle tapping request on the rope, or perhaps waving a finger.

Ultimately you're looking for the horse to glide backwards freely, to the end of the rope remaining calm and relaxed and then smoothly re-join you (draw to you) when invited.

Gently working to achieve smooth, willing backward movement

Tip: Draw To Me

This is when you invite the horse to draw to you – conveying to him that being with you is the warmest, calmest and safest place to be. With a gentle invitation of fingertip movements and passive stance, the horse is motivated to respond willingly. Once he reaches you, offer a pause and some moments of quiet contemplation as a reward. Here, the horse is safe, protected and peaceful. The Draw To Me, along with the Send Away forms the basis for liberty work. This can all be established on-the-line and then perfected at liberty. You can never stop improving these interactions – it is always possible to be softer, clearer, smoother and more subtle in your requests.

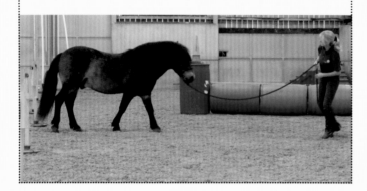

Exercise Seven – Circling

After moving the horse in all of these various directions in the **Core Connection Warm-up Exercises One to Six**, they can now be put together – to create circling. When I request that a horse circles around me, I'm looking for mindful, willing, relaxed steps. I'm not looking for him to scat away and rush around me or use dramatic energy. Because the point of this exercise is to tune into each other and achieve connection with a strong foundation of trust – and focus. In that frame of mind, we're ready for agility and liberty work – and from there energy and speed can safely increase and be managed.

Standing in front of the horse, gently open your left hand and arm, lifting the rope out to the left – radiating your intention that you would like him to yield away from you and move out onto a circle. Invite him to walk around you with a slight bend in his body so he can stay on the circle – neither crowding you or pulling away. The lead rope should have a relaxed 'smile in the line' – it's not there to control him or keep him on the circle. To change direction, gently point to his quarters with your right hand, radiate your intention and ask the horse to yield his quarters away so he comes around to face you again, smoothly and calmly. As that happens, swap the rope from your left to right hand, open your right arm, and ask him to step out and yield away onto the opposite circle – guiding him around you with your right hand.

It can take a bit of practice to achieve smooth, flowing circles and direction changes. This gives the horse the tools and understanding to complete agility obstacles like making figure of eight movements around drums, or moving away to go around something and come back to you. This exercise also offers an

Asking for a circle

Mirroring each other on the line

Mirroring each other at liberty

excellent opportunity to observe any physical or emotional stiffness or blockages – and enables you to gently work through them.

You are now putting all of the Warm-up exercises together to achieve whole body movement – with sending, drawing, bending, yielding – encompassed in the circling and changes of direction.

The point of these exercises is to achieve all this in harmony and in a relaxed and calm manner. When you stand together at the end of a good warm-up session you have reached a place of real core connection. This peaceful and safe place is where you will ask the horse to return to after each agility exercise, or out riding. It is your ultimate safety zone.

Exercise Eight – Mindful Walking together – and Mirroring – to build Connection
After the Warm-up Exercises, you can put your connection to the test and walk about with your horse – on a loose rope or at liberty. The purpose of this exercise is to feel and explore how tuned into each other you are. If it's good, the horse will mirror your movements. You can walk very slowly, then stop, walk on and walk a little faster, slow down again, turn and change direction and stop, then perhaps trot and either return to walk, or put in a halt. This should be done in a way that's clear and fair to the horse, with smooth requests giving him the opportunity to draw, yield away, mirror your paces and stop with you. Half a tonne of horse can feel as light as a feather next to you. It makes a huge difference when showing a pony in hand if you've refined the Warm-up Exercises. And it enables smooth and accurate completion of agility tasks like the canter weave and hoop jumps.

You now have a good set of connection and directional tools for agility and liberty work. It's just a matter of introducing obstacles and tasks to complete.

Chapter 11

Going for Gold and Bear's First Year of Agility Competition

The Positive Effects of the Core Connection Warm-up Exercises

These exercises have positively changed our life and I have come to value them immensely.

Both Bear and I arrive at a training session in various states of mind. He has a vast range of emotions and responsibilities, particularly with regard to his mares, and I'm subjected to the normal trials and tribulations of every day life. Whatever we've been doing and however we are feeling, these mindful and gentle exercises help Bear and me to tune into each other, quieten our emotions and focus. They are brilliant before riding out on the trail and essential to achieving good agility and liberty results. How I wished I had known all about this when I was backing Bear to saddle!

The First Year of Horse Agility Competition

During the first year of Horse Agility competition in 2011, Bear and I were on the steepest learning curve. Although we already had a good basic foundation in groundwork, agility was a whole new world. I could hardly believe that it would be possible to get a horse to navigate around a course of obstacles at liberty and at first, it did seem like an impossible dream. Bear proved to be a magnificent teacher. Formidable, highly-sensitive and with a great sense of self-preservation. 'If you want me to open up to you, then you'd better shape up yourself,' was the message that was coming through loud and clear.

Working with Stallions

With their enhanced intelligence, natural responses and behaviours, handlers need to remain mindful and respectful when working with stallions. At liberty, Bear was invited and able to express exactly how he felt about anything I asked him to do and we were pretty much on equal terms. That could

Getting a horse to navigate obstacles at liberty seemed like an impossible dream at first

Opposite page: Bear with his NPS Gold Medal Rosette after standing Reserve Supreme Champion of the NPS/ Kilmannan Stud Mountain & Moorland Silver Medal Rosette Championship Final in 2011

Working with stallions has an added dimension

be formidable at times. However, it also proved to be amazing and rewarding – and led to greater understanding, softness and acceptance on both our parts. Through giving him his freedom, we learned a great deal about each other. Fear receded and our confidence in each other grew.

Why Getting Excited is the Last Thing Your Horse Wants You to Do

When something good happens that exceeds your expectations, it is natural for us humans to get excited and want to lavish praise on whoever has helped us to achieve this. When we began liberty horse agility and Bear achieved a task, like walking over a see-saw or going over a jump on his own, I would want to praise him.

'That's fantastic Bear, good boy! Good Boy! Well done – Good Boy!' My excitement buzzed away along with my joyful laughter when he'd achieved something new or special. What fun this was! What Bear saw was an alarming rise in my adrenaline, along with my energy, and an erratic, over-excited handler – and he would want to nip me and subdue me. I just didn't understand this for a while and found myself getting an altogether different sort of butterflies feeling when Bear did something amazing at liberty, then turned and would march across the school towards me, with a less than pleasant look on his face. If I'm being honest, he'd sometimes look annoyed and would wave his nose at me like he wanted to bite me.

'Just STOP that!' he seemed to be conveying.

I'd then have to wave my arms and say 'No Bear – Go back!' What was going on?

Well, what was going on was that I was betraying Bear's trust by getting excited. I discovered the crux of the problem – and the solution – by feeling naturally inclined to walk about with Bear calmly after these incidents, gently mirroring each other's movements and then pausing, standing quietly and breathing deeply – and returning to a place of peace and safety. I instinctively realised that this was what Bear needed from me all the time. He didn't want to see me excited – any time ever. Especially when he'd just found the courage to do something new or challenging that required him to try to manage his own adrenaline. When he'd completed the task and was returning to me, he wanted to return to that place of safe, peaceful calmness. Not an adrenaline-high handler. That was just plain annoying – and unsafe.

I realised that Bear took all of this very seriously. He was interested in agility, for sure, but there was a way of conducting ourselves when doing it. If I wanted to work with a stallion at liberty, then I

From top: Bear showing he finds my laughing alarming;
Bear using his ears to convey concentration;
Bear showing his annoyance

had to learn more about the language of The Horse.

It took me the best part of that first year of agility competition to get all this straight in my head, and it's an ongoing process to develop the finesse and understanding of each other to achieve improved 'flow'. Going hand in hand with keeping calm and not showing excitement - was understanding the distinct difference between adrenaline and energy - and learning how to manage the two.

Energy Up/Adrenaline Down

Completing various agility tasks and challenges requires the raising of energy, without activating an alarming rise in adrenaline. A clear trigger of an unwanted adrenaline rush is a handler who asks the horse to engage in fast, energetic liberty tasks like jumping through hoops and cantering through cone weaves – with a shrieking and over-excited manner – thinking they have to 'push' the horse into faster paces. There are various YouTube videos of 'liberty play' showing the catastrophic effects of annoyed or adrenaline-high horses who just 'flip' and lash out at their over-excited handlers. Yet we also see powerful, majestic horses safely performing high-energy liberty with handlers who understand the importance of remaining clear and calm (check out Frederic Pignon's work and his book *Gallop To Freedom*). Remembering to maintain that precious place of core calmness is the greatest reward you can give your horse – because to that he will always want to return. Remember – **Energy Up, Adrenaline Down**.

Reading Each Other

Reading each other correctly is key in horse training. When a predator is about to attack or a scary situation occurs, it is natural to sharply draw in and even hold the breath. A horse reads this in the human as imminent danger, fear or a precursor to the human losing their temper. So when we breathe in and out slowly and deeply, we are communicating that all is well and we are in control of our emotions. We are safe. A predator does not 'strike' from a position of having just emptied their lungs.

At all times the horse is looking for reassurance. So when faced with new obstacles, challenges, noise or other unexpected stimulus like a moving surface, Bear looked to me to read my body language and state of mind. By breathing slowly and deeply, pausing and even giving a sigh, I was able to communicate that all was well, and it was safe to interact with a particular situation. Over time, his capacity for calmly assessing and problem solving – and working out what to do – increased immeasurably. I could see him evolving, developing and becoming receptive to agility training.

Making Mistakes

Throughout the first year of agility, I made many mistakes in the way I asked Bear to do things – and he made sure I was aware of this. If I was clumsy, unclear, or in his opinion, unreasonable with my requests, he would literally throw his hooves up and flounce off, or walk purposefully away. It was quite obvious that he was saying 'Gah!' and I would feel quite chastened. We'd pause, I'd think about what I'd done wrong and Bear would ponder life elsewhere before at some point, coming back to me. We'd reconnect and have another go. Smaller mistakes were met with a frustrated look and a nipping gesture and each time, when I thought about it – it usually transpired that there was a reasonable explanation for his irritation or frustration. These sessions enabled me to significantly improve self awareness, spatial awareness, timing and patience. I valued Bear as a teacher and in turn, he was also learning to become more tolerant – and trusting – of me. We learned from our mistakes and this is ongoing.

Liberty Agility Competition

Each month during 2011 we completed an agility course 'on the line' – using a head collar or halter and 10ft or 12ft lead rope. There were also various liberty agility classes. At first, our liberty efforts were stilted and awkward compared with the entries of more experienced and accomplished competitors and we were low in the placings. However, by continuing to learn, practice and watch other people, we got better.

Liberty Walks to Improve Liberty Competition Performance

I took Bear for some wonderful walks around the farm to develop our liberty connection. We went from field to field, spending as much time as possible with him loose. When I first let him go in a large field, he galloped off to the other side and began grazing. He appeared to be disconnected from me. I wandered over to the stream, sat under a beautiful tree and waited. It took some time, but he gradually worked his way nearer, grazing here and there, until he came back to me. On liberty walks, there is 'horse time' and 'human time' – where horses like to stop, explore, graze and sometimes release bursts of energy. It was important for me not to 'get at him' by making him come with me and going at my pace. I wanted to understand his timescales and behaviours – when he chose to stay with me, what he did when he left me, and when and how he chose to come back to me. Sometimes, once I had got a good distance away from him, such as right across a field, he would raise his head, stare at me and then gallop like a bullet to me, past me and to the gate of that field. With massive energy. At these times, I'd stay where I was and wait. He would turn to stare at me, think about things and then make a conscious choice to return to me – at which point we would walk to the gate together. He was understanding that in order to go through the gate, he needed to connect with me. I started to learn how to communicate my feelings to him without the 'control' of a rope. We were understanding and responding to each other at liberty. The feeling was exhilarating and I now knew to remain calm, and breathe. We could really explore our connection in these big open spaces. The powerful gallops across the field soon became 'to me' rather than 'past me'. Out here, I began to see a more gregarious and playful Bear.

Top: Bear with Georgia and Tambora

Above: Maisie guiding Elbrus

Two More Beautiful Foals

April and May of 2011 brought two beautiful new foals. A filly, Holtball Tambora and a colt, Holtball Krakatoa. This year, the foals would live in a family herd with Bear, who showed great interest, tolerance and softness with the youngsters. The role a stallion plays in the upbringing of foals is one that is rarely seen, as not many have the opportunity to be at the birth of their foals and live with them until weaning time. Bear continued to present us with fascinating learning opportunities through enabling us to study the interactions within a family herd.

Watching Wild Stallions with Foals in Free-living Herds

The involved and interactive role that the stallion plays within a family herd can also be observed with the free-living herds of Exmoor National Park. There can be a distinct difference in the behaviours of mares running with and without a stallion. Without the stallion present, the mares can be more inclined to split up and graze in small bunches, away from each other – and can be more reactive and sensitised to outside stimulus. When a stallion arrives, he will round them all up from the farthest reaches of his enclosure, sometimes spanning hundreds or even thousands of acres, and keep them in a more cohesive, connected herd, even if spread out. After the drama of the initial introductions, there is a calmness present when a stallion is resident in the herd. The stallion will focus on spending time with the mares who are in season, and he also spends time with the foals.

Foals will always approach him carefully, making the submissive mouthing gestures and looking to sniff nostril to nostril to ensure he is accepting of them. When feeling inclined, he will let them jump up on him and play about, mirroring his behaviours. Stallions are very interactive with foals, teaching, playing, over-seeing and generally giving the mares a break from their duties and some 'time off'. When mares and a stallion are able to raise foals together, there is without doubt a sharing of responsibility. The lead mares tend to decide where the herd grazes, and the stallion may be treated 'robustly' by the mares at times, but he certainly appears to be a protecting and calming influence.

The wild stallions will fiercely guard their moorland enclosure boundaries and can be observed squaring up to stallions running in adjacent areas. Sometimes, more than one stallion runs in the same enclosure and there can be altercations and challenges, with the weaker stallion driven off. Generally, each stallion has his own herd of mares and they give each other space. Sometimes, mares will choose to 'swap' herds and it's a constant challenge for the stallion to keep hold of his mares. Some farmers run the occasional colt on out on the moor to retain his hardiness and see if he'll shape up as a potential stallion. This is being increasingly discouraged in the event that the colt manages to cover mares, which can cause chaos with registration of foals. However, a strong stallion is unlikely to let a colt near to a mare in season. Sometimes, entire colts can escape onto the moorland enclosures or are dumped there by irresponsible and unscrupulous owners and this can cause problems to moorland breeding programmes if they manage to cover mares. This is less likely if a resident stallion is present, but makes mares vulnerable to unwanted coverings if not. A great deal is being done to keep the moors clear of unwelcome visitors and we have seen much improvement in recent years through the work of the Moorland Exmoor Pony Breeders Group (MEPBG).

The Mare/Foal Relationship

The foal's dam (mother) tends to be very tolerant of her own foal, guiding and nurturing rather than admonishing. She puts up with a lot of gregarious and sometimes questioning and challenging behaviour as her foal explores, learns and develops. It is the 'aunts' in the herd who are more likely to chastise and make it very clear to a foal who is not their own, when that foal has overstepped the mark – and they can be quite forthright. This is the same with both free-living and in-ground kept breeding herds.

Bear's Response to Exploring Agility Objects with his Foals

This year, Bear and his herd had access to the agility obstacles from their field, so the foals had the opportunity to explore them. We sometimes found them asleep next to the various obstacles, climbing onto the podium, or pawing at the tarpaulin. It was a wonderful way for them to get used to all kinds of shapes, colours and stimulus and it was heartening to see how Bear would play with them in and around the obstacles – standing on the podium or the tarpaulin as if encouraging his foals to do the same – which they did. When given the choice to interact with the obstacles of his own free will – Bear wanted to play with them. He was more relaxed this year – accepting and understanding when leaving his mares and foals to 'do his work' – and returning to them calmly.

Top: Herd 23 free-living stallion The Aristocrat with one of his youngsters

Above: Foals happily resting amongst the agility obstacles

The Contrast Between Agility and Ridden Development with Bear

At seven years old Bear was showing considerable aptitude in his agility training. Hacking out was fun. However, he was not straightforward to ride and whether hacking, schooling or at a competition, he could suddenly produce bursts of hair-raising canter or a fairly immoveable 'plant' if he felt uncertain about something. He had enormous strength – and will.

He always looked after me though. One day, when riding in some large arable fields with bridleways around the perimeter, a ewe had somehow got herself on the wrong side of a wire fence and suddenly chose to make a loud and frantic attempt to get back into her field. This caused Bear to dramatically spook sideways, which had me lurching out of the saddle. Facing onto a wide open space, it would have been natural for him to bolt away from the 'scary situation'. However, as he felt me leaving the saddle, he hesitated and shifted back across to keep me onboard – and then he stopped. Both our hearts were pumping but I felt safe – he did not want me to fall off.

However, to progress with ridden showing, we needed more consistent paces and style and so I sought the advice of some expert trainers from both the Classical and Natural horsemanship worlds. Wide-ranging advice and suggestions included lunging in side reins, using draw reins, various training bits and spurs. I listened to everything, attended some clinics, had some lessons, watched and learned, and tried what I thought was appropriate – avoiding approaches involving obvious force and coercion. For me, harsh bits, spurs and draw reins were not on the menu. I had some excellent help from Rodrigo da Costa Matos from the Portuguese School of Equestrian Art at his UK clinics and I travelled to Portugal for some training on the beautiful Morgado Lusitano stallions. I also had some great assistance from our excellent and empathetic local riding instructor Julie Langrish, who trained at Porlock Vale and instructs the West Somerset Riding Club members.

However overall, I felt there was a chasm developing between the trust, understanding and willing interactions we were evolving with liberty and agility activities – and the way I was expected to be training and riding Bear in the traditional disciplines and competitions.

Another Silver Medal

At the National Pony Society Devon Area Show that summer, Bear stood Overall In Hand Mountain and Moorland Champion and was awarded an NPS Silver Medal, which meant he had qualified for the M&M In Hand Silver Medal Championship Final at the NPS Summer Championships that August.

Going for Gold at the NPS Summer Championships

Bear was full of presence and energy at the NPS Summer Championships. For the NPS/Kilmannan Stud In Hand Mountain and Moorland Silver Medal Rosette Championship Final the winners from across the country are divided into three classes – Big Breeds, Small Breeds and Youngstock. Just being there amongst such beautiful finalists was an honour in itself.

Bear enjoying the cross country course and hacks out

The liberty training had established better understanding with Bear and I was now able to give him his head in the ring, so he could power into his trot without feeling 'restrained'. We had an altogether improved show. In the line up Bear stood proud as if he knew his best behaviour was very important today. We were thrilled to win the Small Breeds section and I hoped we could produce the same level of performance in the final selection, from which the judge, Mr Peter Boustead, would pick the Overall Silver Medal Champion and Reserve Champion. A stunning Fell pony was called forward as Champion and then the steward gestured to Bear to come forward as Reserve Champion. As he handed each of us an NPS gold medal rosette, he said, 'Well done, we don't give many of these out.' It was a moment to cherish.

Trouble on the Way Home

On the way home, however, there was more reason to be proud of Bear. A bearing sheared on our trailer near Bridgwater. With only three wheels functioning properly, we were fortunate to be very close to a farmer friend of Nick's, who arranged to meet us in his nearby field with a stock trailer. Bear would need to swap trailers for the remainder of the journey. Expecting to be at home where he could roar off to see his mares, Bear was decidedly nonplussed to find himself unloading in a strange field full of haylage bales and, staring at him from across a rhyne, a large herd of black cows. With the illusion that they were all in the same field, Bear grew to his full height. Thinking of that place of calmness, we paused and breathed – and he walked straight up inside the stock trailer. The benefits of our agility training were becoming evident when put to the test in an unexpected situation.

The Annual Exmoor Pony Breed Show at Exford Show

Not showing in hand this year, we entered Bear in the Novice and Open Ridden classes at the Exmoor Pony Breed Show. It was a windy day and the Exford Show site, high on the hills of Exmoor, was bracing. Already aware of 'ringcraft' from various competitors after riding Harry, I was nevertheless caught out by one rider who delivered a hearty slap to Bear's rump while we were waiting for the class, which made him leap forwards.

'Oh sorry, there was a fly,' she smirked.

The Novice class was large, Bear gave a nice show and we finished high in the placings. The lap of honour involved a spritely canter, with the ponies keen to leave the ring and the gusting wind adding to the excitement, I could sense the rise in collective energy. As everyone speeded up, I asked Bear for a half halt to steady him but this was rather like trying to stop a cork leaving a champagne bottle. The energy had to go somewhere and I was treated to a spectacular Bear explosion. There was no sitting this for me I'm afraid and off I flew. With a mature Exmoor stallion loose in the ring, it rapidly emptied of exhibits. Getting up, I gestured to people to please not approach Bear and stood quietly, gently asking him to draw to me. He did. He hadn't used the opportunity to gallop off with the other

Top: Bear winning the NPS
Silver Medal Rosette in Devon

Above: Bear winning the NPS
Gold Medal Rosette

Bear and Dawn at the Exmoor Pony Breed Show

ponies. Forgetting that I'd just been bucked off in front of everyone at the breed show, I was very pleased with him. Retaining a strong liberty connection in such a situation is the ultimate goal, particularly with a stallion.

We left the ring to dust ourselves off and had a few minutes before the Open Ridden Class started.

'You're not going back in are you?' said a friend. 'You've got grass stains.'

'Oh yes I am. So important to get back on, so he doesn't think he can just pitch me off like that.' I said, climbing back on board, complete with grassy streaks along my jodphurs. There was no time to change.

Back in the ring we went, to somewhat raised eyebrows from the judge and steward.

This time Bear produced another nice go around that saw him placed high in the line up, followed by a pleasing show with a good trot on the lead change. However, he put in a little buck at the start of the gallop, which caused the judge to put him down the line a couple of places. Nevertheless, we once again finished respectably in the placings. I dispensed with the half halt in the lap of honour and this time we left the ring in the more usual manner. It had been a lively but progressive outing.

Opposite page: Bear relaxed riding bareback and bitless

Right: Bear on the far right with Harry next to him on our 2011 Holt Ball Ride

Bits and Bitless – the Contrast with Bear

As 2011 progressed, so my rapport with Bear deepened. We started exploring the agility obstacles ridden, often bareback with just the halter and a rope. I noticed that when I rode Bear like this he was relaxed and happy. He was letting me know that he liked being ridden without a bit. During the latter part of the year, I often rode Bear out and about in just the Dually head collar, or a halter – and sometimes bareback around the farm. A contrast was emerging between conventional ridden schooling and the bitless riding approach we were experiencing through agility. He let me vault on and off, trotted and cantered along beside me at liberty, and he was fun to ride – responsible, relaxed and reliable. He felt great without a bit and this was something I wanted to evolve.

Bear Takes the Lead

One day, after a particularly good agility session, I decided to sit on Bear with no tack at all. There was a small jump amongst the agility objects. I was just thinking that I'd love to be able to jump him completely tackless, but I simply didn't have the courage – when Bear took matters into his own hands. It was uncanny – he walked forwards, turning around to face the jump, then trotted into it and we jumped it. Then he stopped. We paused and it was like he was saying, 'See – you can do this. I will look after you.' With no prompting from me, he once again walked around the school, broke into a trot, jumped it – and then stopped. It felt great. It was a special moment when I knew that there was immense trust and communication building between us. Bear was proving to be an outstanding teacher.

Competition Heats up in the First International Horse Agility World Championship League

As the agility competition progressed, we moved from Starter level, through Medium to Advanced level, gathering points in the on-the-line and liberty agility classes, which all contributed to the annual total. After the final competition in December, we would know who would be the first International Horse Agility World Champion. There were competitors from the UK, New Zealand, Australia, Europe, USA and Canada. As the year drew to a close, three of us were neck and neck with our points – and there was not yet a clear winner. Everything would hang on the results of the final classes in December.

The Dreaded Balloons

Bear finding the courage to burst a balloon in his December 2011 horse agility class

When the December course was announced, I saw that Bear would be required to burst a balloon with his foot. While there had been much improvement in his confidence, he could still say a resolute 'NO!' to certain things. For example, it had taken infinite patience and tiny steps to convince him that large balls were acceptable. We were still working on that when the balloon bursting task arrived. He had to burst it and remain calm when it went BANG! Bear would need to complete the nine other obstacles in the course perfectly and then burst a balloon with his foot to stand a chance of winning the world championship. We had just over three weeks to prepare.

When I first showed Bear a balloon he took off across the schooling area to the far end, snorting loudly. Balloons were clearly not his thing. To gauge how much of this was Bear and how much was the concept of balloons, I introduced Otis (same age as Bear) and Harry to some balloons and let them explore. The gentle breeze in the barn caused them to float about and Harry wasn't too keen on these strange objects. Otis on the other hand was immediately absorbed with them and walked up and stamped on one. It burst with a loud Bang. He looked pleased and burst another one. Otis gets great satisfaction in dismantling things and the fact that this object which he'd just broken, made a loud noise as well, was immensely enjoyable for him. Minot the Jack Russell terrier could burst multiple balloons in nano-seconds if he spotted them before I spotted him. So, it was just a matter of attitude then!

Over the next couple of weeks, balloons became part of Bear's every day life. They were tied in bunches in the barn and scattered around the floor area. If the JRT found them, he burst them, so Bear began to get used to both the balloons and the noise. I got him to accept putting his foot onto a plastic bag with a little air inside. Then some very sad balloons, blown up a few days earlier, with a pathetic amount of air inside, which made a dismal 'Phut' noise when they burst – building up to the 'Bang!'.

We were getting somewhere, but the entry deadline was approaching. I saw videos of other trainers effortlessly teaching their horses to target a mat with a balloon tied onto it and bursting it, without batting an eyelid. Otis didn't even need a mat. But Bear didn't want to target anything with a balloon on it – any time ever.

I was also not too happy about teaching a stallion to strike out and burst something with his front foot. Bear has never used his front feet to strike out at me, and rearing and striking out 'for fun' are not things I'm personally comfortable about encouraging in training. Stallions do plenty of that in the pasture. Bear was learning to do masses of different and clever things and was becoming responsive and considerate. So I felt we could do without it.

Instead, we came to a mutual agreement that he would tolerate walking through some balloons – and calmly burst one. Walking forwards, he was ultra careful to never put his foot on one. However, he would then accept slowly and purposefully walking backwards, until he burst a balloon with his hind foot. His expression told me that this was a great gesture on his part. Bursting a balloon was a very serious matter indeed for Bear. There was no question of me getting excited about it. A carrot was calmly offered and accepted, and Bear returned to his mares.

Managing Pressure and Staying True to Good Horsemanship

The December entry deadline was now looming and we really needed to film the course. With the world championship at stake there was some inevitable pressure. It was also a real horsemanship test. If I was thinking about the 'prize' of winning and allowed myself to feel the pressure, then I could be sure that Bear would pick this up, and he could well become agitated with me and not give his best performance. That was not good horsemanship. We had the on-the-line course to complete, which finished with the balloon bursting. We then had a completely different liberty course to build, which thankfully had no balloon bursting, but required the completion of about eight obstacles, including throwing a large ball over Bear and jumping through a hoop. We had to do exceptionally well in both classes to win the world championship.

Staying relaxed and enjoying agility must take precedence over competitive ambition

So I had to forget what was at stake, be relaxed and enjoy it. There was no question of trying repeatedly to complete it, because that just doesn't work – and both horse and handler get stressed. So we really did only have two or maybe three opportunities to film a credible entry. Bear completed the first nine obstacles well and we started to walk through the balloons. I would be lying if I said I wasn't feeling a little apprehensive and I did my best to channel that away. Bear was staring solemnly at me.

'I don't like balloons,' he seemed to be saying.

'If you pull this off Bear, I will personally eradicate this property of balloons,' I endeavoured to convey to him. Trying not to hold my breath, I asked him to start walking backwards. There was a reassuring bang. He held his composure with a slight start. Our entry was complete (there is a YouTube video).

All in the Hands of the Cameraman Now

There was a tense couple of minutes while Nick and I replayed the video camera to check the course had been filmed OK. It is not unheard of for the camera person to film an entry while mistakenly on

'standby'. This was not the day to do that. Thankfully, it was all there. I also had to ensure I transferred the footage to the computer and uploaded it correctly, as it's not unheard of for me to mistakenly delete the footage irretrievably during this process. There were plenty of ways to mess it up, practically and technically!

Now we only had the liberty entry to do. We'd have a go at this the following day. The very last day it was possible to put an entry in. In other words, we'd either do it or we'd have no entry.

The Penultimate Liberty Entry for the 2011 World Championship

We set up the liberty course and this was the day when our partnership would be tested to the full. Bear had to complete eight obstacles at liberty wearing a tinsel garland. Firstly he stood still while I threw a large 2ft diameter ball over his back to bounce on the ground beside him. We then walked to the podium which he climbed up onto. Then a walk through a Scary Corner decorated with all kinds of Christmas paraphernalia. Over the See-Saw, through the Plastic Ribbon Curtain, into trot and over the tarpaulin and over a jump. Then back to walk, across the school, around the podium and into a trot for the jump through the Giant Hoop and a calm finish. We did it (there is also a YouTube video). It was hard not to get excited after Bear achieved this. He got a big hug and was well aware of how pleased we were with him.

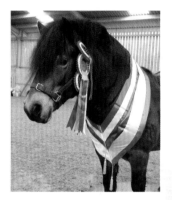

The First International Horse Agility World Champion is Announced

The entries were submitted and everyone waited to see who would win the first International Horse Agility World Championship. It was impossible to tell. When the results were announced, Bear and I had won the annual league by just three points. An extremely close call. The feeling was amazing.

Here was the wild born Exmoor colt, unwanted as a foal, who became champion of his breed in showing and a licenced working stallion – and who had now beaten horses and ponies from across the world in a new equestrian sport that required him to compete at liberty. It was a fantastic achievement for any horse or pony – let alone a moorbred Exmoor pony stallion. It was also a great way to positively promote the endangered Exmoor pony breed and encourage positive, trust-based horsemanship. BBC Spotlight came to film us and the attributes and qualities of Exmoor ponies were promoted far and wide. For me, this was the primary motivation for taking part in a competition that spanned twelve continuous months. We received £250 in prize money and some new agility equipment. It had been an amazing experience.

Opposite page: Bear and Dawn stand 2011 International Horse Agility World Champions

Chapter 12

Success Through Overcoming Adversity

Straight into Another Horse Agility League Competition

The 2012 Agility League started right away. This year there were also Wild Agility classes which would involve completing natural obstacles and tasks in open spaces.

I was intrigued to see if Bear could work at liberty out in a natural environment as well as in the school. We still had a lot to learn and so we decided to take part for another year. Looking around the farm, we found areas of woodland and rougher ground that would make the perfect environment for developing wild agility skills. There ideally needed to be a stream, rough undergrowth to navigate through, natural obstacles to jump over and trees to weave through.

The 2012 agility courses would require faster paces

Preparing for Faster Paces in Agility

Bear's agility skills were progressing and we were learning how to raise and lower our energy, without alarming rises in adrenaline. It was all work in progress and the learning curve was still steep. The agility courses were becoming harder and more complex and a faster pace would be required in this coming year, with increased trotting and the introduction of tasks at canter. One of the tasks was a Canter Weave which, to do smoothly, required flying changes all the way down the line of cones.

With Bear at eight years old, I had to make choices regarding what to focus on. Although we would certainly continue to progress his ridden work, the agility competition would require many courses to be built, learned, completed and filmed throughout the year – requiring considerable time and resource. Agility had the potential to massively benefit native ponies and evolve as a new equestrian sport, so we decided to put our efforts behind both competing and promoting it. Serious ridden showing was therefore set aside for another year.

Bear navigating a
Wild Agility challenge

Bear and his filly foal
Holtball Isla Isabel

Two Beautiful Filly Foals

2012 brought us two beautiful fillies, Holtball Mayon and Holtball Isla Isabel. Bear had settled well into this little family herd with Maisie and Georgia and was able to happily balance stud life with his performance activities.

Our Other Exmoor Ponies

Although there's not much room here to talk about our other Exmoor ponies, it's worth noting that agility was also proving to be helpful with ponies like Harry and Otis. They were being ridden regularly and the agility activities helped their confidence and enjoyment. Harry proved to be outstanding riding the agility courses – and both ponies have since progressed to bitless riding. Horse agility is a great way to get the young ponies used to all kinds of shapes, colours and experiences – making it much easier when it comes to backing them to saddle. Bear's son Monty particularly enjoyed it and had progressed to Advanced level.

Agility Demos

From late 2011 and through 2012, Bear and I took part in some public horse agility demos for the agility competition organiser. We started with a demo at the South West Christmas Equine Fair, where Bear's responses were as electric as the atmosphere – the spectators might easily have believed he had come off the moor only the day before! There was a distinct difference between performing at home and performing in front of a large crowd of people in a strange place. Somehow, we had to bridge that gap. Things progressed and there was success at the Bath & West Game Fair, when after a nice demonstration of the agility obstacles on the rope, the commentator asked if I could turn Bear loose. The ring was outside and constructed with just a single strand of tape. A shooting demonstration was taking place nearby and both adults and children were milling around everywhere. I unclipped Bear and we navigated some obstacles, finishing with a jump through the hoop. He stayed calm and came back to me. We were really getting somewhere.

The Hot Branding Debate Smoulders On

Alongside the highs of winning the horse agility world championship and Bear's showing success, the hot branding debate continued. The Animal Welfare Act 2006 and the 2007 Permitted Mutilations Regulations (England) made it clear that no unnecessary suffering should be caused to animals, and the equine charities, veterinary associations and various government representatives discussed and debated the issues. However, the message had been conveyed that change and welfare improvement for Exmoor ponies was needed.

Bear Joins the Police

We are fortunate to have a proactive police force in Avon and Somerset which has pioneered a Rural Mounted Watch scheme to enlist the help of local horse riders to patrol rural areas. In order to join the team, horse and rider have to pass a designated riding test, after which they are kitted out in high-visibility gear, ready to patrol during their hacks out. Wouldn't it be great if an Exmoor pony stallion, born wild and free on the moor could join them? We had to demonstrate that Bear could be ridden at all paces in an open field and then stand quietly if I needed to get off and tend to a situation from the ground. We passed the test and it was quite something to see Bear riding out as a Rural Mounted Watch team member.

Success at Royal Cornwall in 2012

With our focus firmly on horse agility this year, Bear's only showing outing was a trip to Royal Cornwall where he stood Champion Exmoor for the third time. We almost didn't go as there was a severe gale with many trees down *en route*. The wind can be rather 'fresh' at Royal Cornwall Showground and on this occasion it had people hanging onto their hats with airborne objects routinely flying past. This created a rather more lively atmosphere than usual but Bear coped well. We were, however, very glad to get home safely.

Above: Bear joins the Avon and Somerset Police Rural Mounted Watch Team

Right: Champion Exmoor at Royal Cornwall Show 2012

BBC Spotlight on Hot Branding

In June, we featured in a BBC Spotlight news story about Multiple Hot Branding and the welfare issues resulting from its continued practice – enabling the plight of the ponies to receive some much needed publicity. A petition organised by a concerned vet calling for Multiple Hot Branding of domestic ponies in England & Wales to stop, attracted over 13,000 signatures in just a few weeks. The press picked up the story. The subject of Multiple Hot Branding was discussed at the highest levels in Government. Things were beginning to positively progress.

Horse Agility Summer of Sports Championship Final and an Attack on Bear

Within the Horse Agility Competition for 2012 was a separate Summer of Sports Championship and Bear qualified for the final. This required him to complete a challenging course culminating with him climbing onto a podium and, after a pirouette, accepting a decorative garland over his head. Under ordinary circumstances this would not have been a problem as Bear had grown accustomed to having all kinds of things over his head – flags, reins, rugs, etc. So I hadn't given it a second thought. Except that a few weeks before the final entry deadline, Bear was assaulted in his field which resulted in him being left with some trauma-related behaviours.

That summer had brought a raft of midges and with the mares and foals keen to chew at Bear's mane, I'd put a fly sheet on him during the worst few weeks. Bear's sheet did up with multiple fastenings. One morning I found him standing inside the barn looking subdued. His mares and foals were with him and their energy told me they were less than happy. Immediately noticing the absence of his fly sheet, I was perplexed. He was a sensitive, feisty Exmoor stallion running with his herd and it would not be easy to catch him in his field at night. So either 'falling out' of his rug, or having someone be able to take it off him – without force – were both highly unlikely.

'How on earth did you get out of that Bear?' I asked him. He just stared at me through his huge forelock. 'That sheet can't just slip off.'

I went out to the paddocks to look for it and couldn't find it. Nick searched for it too without success. However, he did discover clear signs that we'd had an unwelcome visit during the night. I had a good look at Bear, who was not his usual self. He didn't appear to be obviously injured. However, someone had managed to get his rug off and steal it, so something undesired had occurred.

It wasn't until the next day that I experienced some of the psychological effects of Bear's assault. When I'd finished grooming him to prepare for riding and I went to place the reins over his head, he literally exploded. It was reminiscent of his reaction to dummy rider Boris, but this time with a harrowing roar. Bear leapt backwards, breaking the reins, and erupted into a series of leaps and bucks that lasted some time. Finishing over the other side of the barn, he stood with deep furrows above his eyes, looking upset.

'Oh Bear, what have they done to you?'

We later discovered that the jaggedly severed neck and head piece of Bear's fly sheet had been returned to the farm. Picking on Bear showed immense cowardice and a complete disregard for the welfare of the pony. The very essence of the problems we were trying to address.

Dealing with Fear and Anger

The immediate task was to try to overcome Bear's new fear of having anything placed over his head. With the deadline for the Horse Agility Summer of Sports Final entry looming, if I couldn't even place reins over his head, how could I possibly get him to accept the garland?

Anger is not a good emotion at the best of times. It creates negative energy which horses find alarming because, when humans are angry, they can become unpredictable, defensive and dangerous. Horses can read this energy and prefer to stay away from angry humans, for their own safety. Unsurprisingly, Bear's attack had made me angry and that was completely counter-productive to our liberty work. Or indeed any work with Bear and the other ponies – whether day to day handling, agility, riding or showing. With the Exmoor Pony Breed Show just weeks away, we had certainly been set back in all respects. The answer was, of course, not to allow it to set us back.

Recognising my anger as an emotional messenger, I thanked it for alerting me and asked it to recede, channelling the negative energy away to be reabsorbed deep into the earth and re-processed into positive energy. When the anger welled up in me, I acknowledged it and asked it to pass on through. It was a good time to remember Karma – and let the Universe create a balance once again.

Working with Bear, I remembered when I was trying to win the trust of that fearful, highly sensitive young colt and in some respects, I felt I was starting all over again with him. With challenging agility courses to learn and complete imminently – both for the normal monthly league competition and for the Summer of Sports Championship Final – we focused on the elements he enjoyed most, and took everything very gently. In addition to now hating anything being put over his head, he also no longer tolerated the fly spray or mane and tail spray. Spraying anything near his front end had become a No Go Zone. Bear was displaying clear signs of Post Traumatic Stress Disorder.

Bear was decidedly out of sorts after his attack and did not want anything placed over his head – even reins

Overcoming Adversity

So we had quite a bit to work on. For me ensuring that I brought a relaxed, calm and authentic core energy to our training sessions – and to gently work with Bear so he would allow me to place the garland around his neck for the agility entry. We spent much time together just 'being' and I gradually reintroduced the idea of laying things over and around his neck and wither.

We continued to learn the rest of the course and I had to take great care when putting on the bridle as one wrong move would have him leaping backwards. However, we persevered as I wanted to return to normality as soon as possible and not let him build up these new phobias in his mind. We were using Professor Temple Grandin's theories about horses thinking in 'visual slides' and I was endeavouring to layer positive experience 'slides' over the vibrant negative experience – until it faded back in his memory, rather than leaping into his mind at the sight of any stimulus that reminded him of what he'd been through.

Two days before the final entry agility deadline and Bear still didn't want anything lifted up and over his head. I had resigned myself that it would take the time it takes. We'd have a go at filming the course on the final day and if wasn't possible, I wasn't going to lose any sleep over it. The important thing was Bear's peace of mind and we would go at his pace – competition or no competition.

The final day for filming the entries arrived and Bear completed all of the obstacles very well. He then went up onto his podium, did his pirouette and stood there while I picked up the garland. We looked at each other.

'I really need you to trust me Bear. You can do this. Don't let them beat you. I'm not going to let them beat me,' I was thinking.

Bear studied me intently as I lifted the garland and placed it over his head. He stood there without moving or spooking. We had done it. I remembered not express my delight and instead we took a quiet pause. Bear had faced his demons and overcome his phobia. He had the courage of a lion.

Bear overcomes adversity to win Gold and Silver Medals in the Summer of Sports Horse Agility Championship Final

Results of the Summer of Sports Championship Final

It was particularly poignant when the results were announced and Bear and I had won Summer of Sports Gold and Silver Medals. He thoroughly deserved them. Once again I was so proud of him, this time not simply for being talented at the agility, but in managing to overcome some considerable adversity. We were also mid-way through the 2012 Horse Agility League and on course for being contenders for another world championship. The standard was improving across the board and the competition was hot.

Back to our Local Horse Show

This year, Bear's son Monty represented Holtball Herd 11 at our local horse show and he stood both Exmoor and Mountain and Moorland Champion. No heckling, no grabbing of the young stallion and, at last, a friendly and fun day. A rainy start, then bright sunshine – and no chill wind!

The 2012 Exmoor Pony Breed Show

Shortly afterwards, it was time for the Exmoor Pony Breed Show and I'd entered Bear in the Stallion class.

'If he sees anything that worries him, he will likely either explode, or become very subdued, or both,' I said to Nick. 'He certainly won't be his usual sparkly self. Let's see what happens.'

Bear was happy in himself on arrival at the show and had polished up pretty well. I took him through to the familiar collecting area next to the show rings. He felt active and alert walking beside me. Then he exploded, leaping into the air. I followed his gaze to see what had alarmed him. After this, Bear became subdued and rather contrary.

The judge remarked that Bear was not his usual self as she gave him a fourth place rosette.

'I know.' I replied quietly. But we had gleaned useful information from the experience.

The First Exmoor Pony Festival

At the beginning of August, we were visited by the Moorland Exmoor Landscape Partnership (Exmoor National Park Authority), to discuss the possibility of launching the first ever Exmoor Pony Festival to promote the moorbred Exmoor ponies. The idea had been circulating during the year, however nothing had yet been done to organise it – and the aim was to hold the festival at the end of August. This meant we would have less than four weeks to plan, promote and hold it. We were asked if we'd like to host an event and we offered to put on a Liberty and Agility Demo with Bear. We were also asked if we could help with the organisation and promotion of the Festival itself, so August was an extremely busy month. With people and organisations galvanised into action the events started to take shape. The first Exmoor Pony Festival was hailed a success and, with a good crowd packed into our barn at Holt Ball, Bear gave a lovely liberty demo to promote the qualities and trainability of Exmoor ponies.

Wild Agility

Wild Agility was proving to be enormous fun. We were set some really interesting tasks, like asking our ponies to weave through trees; canter alongside us in open spaces showing control of paces; running through jumbled wilderness areas; navigating gateways; crossing water and jumping natural obstacles. It was exhilarating and challenging – and Bear loved it. Playing at liberty and learning new tasks helped him to regain much of the confidence and trust that had been shaken by his assault. Nick took precious time out from farming to traipse around these wild areas with us and capture the footage. It required a bit of practice and more than once, we did a wonderful run only to find a psychedelic blur on the camera, or lovely footage of foliage and sky, as Nick battled with the bright sunlight and dark shadows - with a less than brilliant camera. It wasn't easy but within a very short time, he became an ace wildlife cameraman. I was very grateful for his patience and support. Without him, we could not compete.

A Wild Trip and a Calf in Distress

In order to progress Bear's Wild Agility skills, we took him to a nearby farm which had a large common area adjacent to the moor, with interlocking enclosures grazed by Devon cattle. There was plenty of space for Bear and me to explore our connection. It went very well and on the way back up to the trailer, with Bear still at liberty, he suddenly stared into the distance and took off at a gallop.

'Oh crikey, I hope he hasn't spotted a herd of moorland mares,' I said to Nick, wondering if the boundaries really were secure. Bear galloped up to the top of the enclosure and stood staring over the fence into the next field, while we made our way up the steep track as quickly as possible. Trotting back down the fence line, he darted through the open gate and cantered across to join the herd of Devon cattle.

'Oh God!' I said. Nick, of course, remained calm.

When we reached the enclosure, we could see Bear standing quietly on the other side of the herd, staring back at us.

'Why has he gone over there?' I couldn't really understand his behaviour. He was staring earnestly at us. It was peculiar. He stayed there, not moving. As we made our way over, the cows and calves meandered across the field. There was a small steer calf on Bear's side, around four months old, walking along with his mother. Suddenly he started to look dizzy and uneven on his feet and within a short time, dropped to the ground, leaving his mother in some distress. Bear stood staring at the calf. Nick went across and examined it, perplexed.

'Do you know, and I've never seen it here in all these years, I think this calf has magnesium deficiency. He needs treatment fast.' The calf was now motionless. We had to do something quickly.

'There's no phone signal at all here. We need to drive to a signal and I'll get them to flip out and treat this calf straight away,' said Nick.

Bear was on his best behaviour, coming across the fields with us without a murmur, loading straight away, and we were shortly on our way. The calf was where we had left him and looked dead, his stressed mother standing over him.

As soon as we had a signal, Nick phoned the farm and suggested what he thought was the problem and we waited to see if they could reach the calf in time. The call came soon after.

The farmer told Nick that the calf had looked 'as dead as a hammer' but that a few minutes after treating him, he'd got up and was off again, as right as rain.

So Bear had alerted us to this problem and we'd been able to act quickly enough to save the calf. Another feather in the cap of this extraordinary stallion – and my husband's perceptive diagnostics.

Riding Out with Liberty Connection

One of the things I most enjoyed was riding out on the trail with Bear and being able to let him go. If I wanted to get off for any reason, such as opening a tricky gate, I could dismount and attend to it without having to hold him. Sometimes I'd jump off and we'd walk or jog along together in the forest, across a field or out on the moor – with Bear at liberty. It was a wonderful feeling that he wanted to stay with me. At the end of a ride around the fields, I'd dismount and let Bear graze for a while. He would always follow me. He was proving to be the most incredible pony and we enjoyed some fantastic rides out during that season.

Top: Bear alerting us to the calf in distress

Middle, below and opposite: Enjoying riding out and walking with liberty connection

Chapter 13
A Natural Management System

Barefoot Riding

Bear has never been shod. His immensely hard and well-shaped feet have had regular care from farriers and a barefoot trimmer, and this is important when riding out on varied terrain from stony and flinty tracks and tarmac lanes, to fields, forestry and moorland.

How Horses Hooves Work

When a horse's foot is unshod it is able to fully function as nature intended. The hoof is free to expand and contract as it hits the ground then lifts off again as the horse moves. This motion serves as a powerful pump for the circulation system, which results in a warmer horse, and all the benefits good circulation brings. The frog and heel bulbs are able to function properly, with the heel bulbs becoming well muscled. The floor of the hoof becomes strong and well-calloused and is able to cope with different surfaces and a degree of concussion – not bruising as easily as softer, pared away undersoles. The barefoot horse tends to have an immensely strong hoof wall and they can feel and process the surfaces they touch – slippery tarmac, grass, gravel, shingle or sand, stoney and muddy surfaces – and respond and react accordingly. Bear's hooves were rock solid, well-shaped and he could hack out over any terrain – I was just more careful to avoid obviously rough surfaces where possible.

A Natural Management System for Horses and Ponies

Going barefoot is just one aspect of a more natural management system which we believe assists the wellbeing and health of Exmoor ponies, who after all, are used to living wild and free. Out on the moor, they have the benefit of extensive areas to roam, many different surfaces to wear and trim their feet, a wide range of rough vegetation and moorland grasses to eat and plenty of natural shelter –

Free-living Exmoor ponies making the most of natural shelter on the Lynton cliffs from both inclement weather and summer midges and flies. They are also able to remain as nature intended – growing and shedding their coats with the seasons. Exmoor ponies naturally grow an awesome double-layered winter coat, which when combined with their thick manes, forelocks and tails, padded eyes, small ears and strong jaw structure – means they are built to survive all of the harsh conditions that the Exmoor terrain and weather can throw at them. We wanted to learn from all this and try and adapt the conventional domestic stable and paddock environment, where we could, to suit the Exmoor ponies – and indeed the Arabian horses – living on the farm.

There is no doubt that it is easier to prepare and ride a rugged, clipped, stabled horse in the winter, than it is to extract a wet, muddy, hairy native from the field and work out where and how to get a saddle in place amongst the mass of coat – often sodden and plastered in mud. However we're keen for our Exmoors to retain their natural characteristics and behaviours – and hardiness. Particularly when it comes to breeding sires, brood mares and youngstock. What Bear and the other ponies ideally needed was free access to good shelter and pasture – unencumbered by rugs.

Environment, Surfaces and Bedding: The answer for us lay in letting the ponies run in herds and creating barn and shelter environments with various surfaces, such as concrete, compacted chalk or hardcore – and suitable bedding areas of wood pellets or sand. These lead out to open concrete, compacted hardcore or bark-chipped corral areas, which in turn lead out to tracks and pasture areas. The ponies can migrate in and out as they wish. Good quality, alkaline (non-acidic) sea sand is particularly good for their feet and coats and has a naturally antiseptic effect – with the grains able to exfoliate the feet and help to take mud off the legs and coat. Barn/shelter/bed and corral areas are thoroughly skipped out a couple of times daily. Clean living areas mean less likelihood of foot problems and we see very little evidence of abscesses in the feet or mud fever. We chain harrow, rotate and cross-graze the pasture to keep it healthy.

Rugs and Grooming: The use of rugs is kept to a minimum. An active showing or performance pony may need to wear a sheet or light rug at times to protect the coat and mane. A skin sensitive pony will benefit, if kept in ground where midges can be more intense, from fly sheets in the summer months. But other than that, our aim is to allow the ponies to grow, shed and regulate their coats as nature intended. It was normal, in Bear's routine, for him to be washed and groomed the day before, put in a light fly sheet and turned back out with his mares, then brought out of the field in the early hours and taken straight to a show. Many a championship was acquired with very little interference to Bear's natural management system.

Feeding and Nutrition: The ponies are fed good quality forage (hay and haylage), usually in large tractor tyres if they are in a big herd, or on the ground. They have access to low-molassed, quality mineral licks and salt rocks. If necessary, they can be fed a small amount of non-heating, high-fibre feed, with micronised linseed and a Vitamin E & Lysine supplement, or linseed oil – and unmolassed

We provide as natural an environment as possible for the Exmoor ponies

chaff. Happy Tummy Charcoal helps to regulate stomachs if needed. Some ponies will exist very well simply on grass, forage and mineral licks. Forage is available ad lib, as is access to turnout and grazing.

The Mud Wallow: When allowed to live naturally, the horses and ponies will inevitably make or find a mud wallow and can arrive in the barn absolutely plastered in mud. This is a wonderful ritual and it's quite something to watch both them – and sometimes the visiting wild deer – playing and rolling in the wallow. Some ponies like the briefest dip while others will completely cover themselves in mud! They'll also choose – or create – muddy patches in the grass and take it in turns to roll there. This is a way of creating a 'herd scent' and is a very social activity. Sometimes, when I took Bear on liberty walks, he'd find a natural wallow and dive in.

Progress with Multiple Hot Branding

In September 2012, it was decided at an Exmoor Pony Society General Meeting to cease using the Exmoor Pony Star brand – the generic mark applied to the shoulder of foals and to reduce the number of brands to a maximum of four marks, applied to the rump only. Although there was still no move to stop the Multiple Hot Branding of foals coming off or born off the moor, this represented considerable welfare improvement for Exmoor ponies. Nevertheless, the campaign to stop the Multiple Hot Branding of non-moorbred foals needed to continue.

Hot branding finally reduced to the rump only; however, branding of foals born off the moors remained unrestricted

Filly Farleywater Dazzler enjoying the Mud Wallow at Holt Ball – in February!

Chapter 14
A Second Agility World Championship and Ridden Showing

Striving for a Second Horse Agility World Championship

With Wild Agility igniting Bear's enthusiasm and our connection developing well, Bear's liberty work improved immeasurably.

He could now jump confidently through the Giant Hoop at a good height, had an amazing recall when out on liberty walks and was a joy to ride out on the trail. Importantly, when faced with new agility courses and challenges, Bear had 'learned to learn'. I set out the new obstacles and he would follow me around and study things carefully. He waited for me to show him what we were supposed to do – and was able to learn different applications of the same obstacle during the same month. Sometimes, for example, we'd have to navigate a T-Bend in a certain way and at certain paces for the on-the-line course, and in a completely different way for the liberty course. Bear learned to focus, concentrate and work out what was required – and remember it. I found him an amazing partner to work with.

Our goal was to try to win a second world championship in horse agility. With a significant lead of accumulating league points, if we did well in the November classes, it would be possible to win the world championship with a month in hand. We submitted our November liberty and on-the-line entries.

When the Horse Agility competition results were announced at the end of November, it was clear that, even if our nearest competitor won their December class, we had won the annual league by over 100 points. The results were posted on the agility website and people began to congratulate us. We'd done it – a second International Horse Agility world championship for a wild-born Exmoor pony stallion! We were over the moon. As we had been competing for 23 months in a row without a break – and in 21 classes in 2012 alone – I decided not to compete Bear in December. He needed a rest from competitive agility and so did we. It was time to celebrate.

However, unlike other sports leagues, despite the winning results being published on the competition website and congratulations pouring in – no formal announcement was made by the competition organisers. I received a curt email telling me to be quiet about winning the league as

there was apparently 'an advertising strategy'. When the end of December eventually arrived, there was a brief website announcement of the results but no prizes or fanfare this year. The 'advertising strategy' appeared not to include Bear and myself taking any of this limelight with our second horse agility world championship win.

Our drive and motivation to have taken part in the competition was the opportunity to promote the quality and trainability of Exmoor ponies, enhance their image and encourage people to get involved in the sport – with ponies. I had also wanted to show that even wild-born tempestuous stallions can perform willingly – and safely – at liberty. We now had a wonderful, responsive and connected stallion who was acquiring fans for Exmoor ponies across the world.

We had enjoyed taking part for two years. However, it once again appeared to be a little chilly in the top spot and we decided it was time to seek warmer climes. You certainly don't have to be a world champion to to be a winner – agility activities can be enjoyed by everyone, inside and outside of competition. Rudyard Kipling's wonderful poem 'If' was an inspiration to me at this time.

A Return to Ridden Showing

Bear was now nine years old. He was maturing emotionally and physically and feeling good to ride. He had reached the top in both in hand showing and agility. We decided that this was the year to progress his ridden training.

Above: International Horse Agility World Champions for the second year running in 2012

Opposite page: Bear demonstrates the giant hoop jump and cone weaves at liberty

Above: Bear returns to ridden competition in 2013

Left: At the 2013 Exmoor Pony Stallion Parade

Bear showing great tenderness with his colt son Holtball Baluran, who is making gestures of submission and respect to his father

Sam Roberts, one of Britain's top native pony producers and show riders, was also interested in seeing how Bear could do in ridden showing and we arranged to meet her at an indoor school during the winter to ride Bear and see how they got on. Bear was soon trotting and cantering figure of eights and working forwards into a nice outline. She liked him a lot. We arranged to meet when logistics allowed and in the meantime, I could deal with his day to day riding and fitness training.

I took Bear along to the local Riding Club Dressage and Show Jumping events, which combined some excellent tuition with Julie Langrish followed by competitions. We also hacked out and I now had an Australian Light Rider bitless bridle which I alternated with Bear's loose ring snaffle. We attended some Matthew Lawrence ridden clinics - sometimes meeting Sam Roberts there too – and between all of us, Bear made very good progress. He particularly liked his jumping. It was looking promising.

The Exmoor Pony Stallion Parade

In the spring, we once again took Bear to the Stallion Parade and he behaved impeccably. I was able to show him on a long rope with a smile in the line, where he moved with me, turned when I turned, circled around me and followed me. He was wonderful to handle – light, responsive, connected and incredibly proud of himself – and he sparkled. People remarked how lovely it was to see a happy, relaxed stallion, shown without a stick and on a loose line. The heavy stallion bit was a dim and distant memory – as was the Rescue Remedy. Bear was wearing his pony starter bit – and the lead rope was clipped onto the ring under his noseband, rather than onto the bit. Bear's exemplary behaviour at the Stallion Parade showed me that we were without doubt on the right horsemanship path.

Holtball Baluran

May 2013 brought the arrival of a beautiful colt foal, Holtball Baluran. His natural nickname was 'Balu' so finally, I had my 'Baloo'. Balu was our only foal this year and Bear formed a very strong bond with him. Balu adored his father and as soon as his mother Georgia would allow him to interact with Bear, he stuck to him like glue, following him about and trying to emulate his behaviour. Balu always approached Bear with the greatest respect and one day, I saw an amazing interaction between them. After sniffing noses and lowering their heads, Balu actually lay down at his father's feet in total submission. The response of the stallion was to be tender and reassuring – it was moving to watch and I managed to capture it on camera. Bear and Balu spent hours together, patrolling the boundary, standing guard and watching over everything.

Bear's Sheep Herding

Sometimes, when Nick wanted to move sheep to different fields, he suggested that Bear and I came along too. It gave Bear the opportunity to be amongst all the hustle and bustle – whether helping to

Above: It is rare to lose a lamb to foxes or badgers with Bear grazing in the field

Left: Bear learning to herd sheep – here ridden in the Dually head collar

move and direct the sheep, or standing still with them all around him. It was great training and a fun way of developing Bear's ridden skills. He often grazed in fields full of sheep and it was interesting that lambs were very rarely lost to foxes or badgers when Bear was turned out with ewes and lambs.

Devon County Show – Bear's First Ridden Class with his Top Show Rider

That spring, we were excited to take Bear for his first ever County Show ridden class. It would be his debut with Sam Roberts and was an important qualifier for the Exmoor breed. They gave a lovely show and we were delighted at his way of going and good behaviour. Unfortunately, Bear and Sam were awarded fourth place in the ridden class. It was a curiously inauspicious start to the season but nevertheless good experience for Bear.

Bear going beautifully at Devon County with Sam Roberts

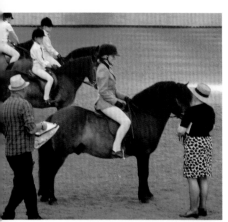

Bear and Dawn winning their
qualifier at the SWPA Show

SWPA Summer Show

We took Bear to a South West Pony Association show where the Mountain and Moorland classes were held in an indoor arena. Bear gave me a lovely ride, standing Reserve NPS Peasedown Champion and 1st Res NPS M&M Silver Medal Champion – and qualifying for the NPS Peasedown Intermediate Final at the NPS Championships in August.

Bear Causes a Stir in a Ridden Qualifier – But Not for Quite the Right Reasons

Due to conflicting schedules with Sam, I was riding Bear myself in this important qualifier. The rain was relentless and after a sodden warm up we made our way to the very smart white picket-fenced show ring, surrounded by marquees and colourful flower displays. Competitors, ponies and judges were top level. It was exciting for us to be amongst them, if a little daunting – for both myself and Bear as it turned out. The go around started well, with a pleasing walk and trot. The steward asked us to canter on and this progressed nicely – although I was aware that Bear was keen to press on. We were directed to change the rein and trot across in front of the judges. All good. Picking up the canter again, I could feel Bear's energy rising and he spurted forwards. I tried a half halt – and felt the cork start to leave the champagne bottle. Riding him forwards out of what might become an explosion, he began to bolt. The feeling was one of putting your foot down on the accelerator of a sports car, when you don't want to go faster. The pony in front loomed up and we were soon past. I tried the usual requests to slow down – relaxing, breathing deeply and asking him to come back to me. I tried easing off the contact and avoiding sitting forwards. I tried left rein pressure with my inside leg on. Nothing worked. We were bolting.

A famous show rider asked if we were OK as we overtook her at a fair rate of knots.

'Not really' I muttered.

As we gathered speed and it became apparent that we were perhaps putting just a little too much effort into our canter, we caught the attention of the stewards and judges, who had been comfortably spaced out in the middle of the ring studying the ponies. Nothing was working to persuade Bear to slow down and he felt like he was gearing up to jump out over the picket fencing, so I increased my left rein and inside leg aids and started to make a smaller circle, in the hope that he'd understand my desire to 'b***** slow down.' Well the circle got smaller, but the speed was maintained. The feel was now more 'motorbike' than sports car. The increasingly alarmed officials started retreating into a defensive 'bunch', a little like a circle of wagons under attack – and Bear finally spun to an abrupt halt - with his neatly herded judges and stewards 'gathered'.

'No Bear, they're not sheep!' I whispered to him.

A word from the judge caused the steward to ask everyone to line up. The 'go around' had been brought to an abrupt end. As we walked forwards past the wide-eyed officials, I caught the expression on a steward's face – was it me or was he trying to contain an involuntary guffaw?

Left to right: Bear and Dawn starting off well; Bear begins to feel keen to press on; Starting to bolt; bolting

We found ourselves in the middle of the line-up, so Bear had some time to regain his composure before his individual show. In fact, he stood like a statue, as if nothing had happened. I was pretty sure we'd confirmed ourselves in last place – the rest of the class was now about deciding the other placings. Then a little girl on a lovely pony began their individual show and it became evident that Bear was not the only naughty pony in the class today. The pony started with a spritely walk and trot and when asked to strike off in canter, didn't. Despite various repeated requests, no canter was forthcoming, but the trot did get faster. He and his increasingly frustrated rider changed the rein and she asked for the canter on the other leg. No, it was all about trotting today and the pony refused to produce his canter – with aplomb.

'Thank you God,' I found myself thinking, then admonished myself for joining that dreadful bandwagon where 'others must fail too'.

Nevertheless, we now perhaps had a contender for bottom of the line up. After some beautiful shows which indicated who'd be in the top end, it was Bear's turn. But before I had a chance to go forwards, an official came over and said that my pony was a 'little unnerved' today. She asked if I thought we could do anything, anything at all, even a little circle and then return to the line-up.

'Yes, I'm sure we can do something.' It was too embarrassing to be embarrassed so I just smiled.

She agreed that we should do what we could, but pointed out that if Bear repeated what he'd done earlier, they would have to ask us to leave the ring.

My resolve strengthened to get it right. 'I know you can do it Bear.' I thought.

First we had to walk away, then turn and trot back past the judge, and then continue with our usual show of a figure of eight, showing both canter strike-offs, followed by a gallop down one side of the arena, then back to canter, trot, walk and then halt, with a salute. This we duly did. Not a perfect performance, but certainly acceptable. A calm and collected Bear returned to the line up. Then it was off with his tack for the in hand trot up which went well. With everyone eventually remounted, we waited for the scores and final placings. Bear's individual show helped and we found ourselves placed in the final six of the line-up rather than last. Before we left for the lap of honour, one of the judges wagged her finger at Bear and said, '*You* can do this!'

Indeed he could – yet it was not a walk in the park with the magnificent Bear.

A Question of Bits and Whips – and a Quandary

Bear appeared to thoroughly enjoy trail-riding and jumping – particularly when ridden in the bitless bridle – and was less fond of dressage and ridden showing. He could naturally engage and 'round up' – with elevation, cadence and impulsion, with his nose 'just in front of the vertical' – when he wanted to. When he produced this it felt amazing – and effortless – to ride. However, tension of any kind brought a reluctance to go forwards freely. Riding forwards assertively and 'backing up the leg' with the whip would result in Bear moving forwards as directed – but with accompanying resistance. The magic happened when Bear *wanted* to move freely forwards, powering from behind, and it became understandably 'mechanical' if he didn't. Along with putting the brakes on, Bear revealed tension by opening his mouth.

At open level in ridden showing, it is *de rigueur* to wear a Pelham (double bridle with a Pelham bit). So I researched the mildest Pelham I could find, suitable for a pony-sized mouth. The general consensus was that a simple French Link lozenge pony Pelham was worth a try. Bear disliked it and continued to periodically open his mouth.

I experimented at home, sometimes riding out in the loose ring French link 'lozenge' snaffle (a gentle pony starter bit), and at other times, in the bitless bridle. This had no poll pressure and was a simple side pull with a canvas strap running under the chin. When I rode bitless, Bear kept his mouth shut, released his base of neck, relaxed and went forwards with enthusiasm – rounding up, engaging his back end and powering along. He was less relaxed in the snaffle – and least happy in the Pelham. I received advice from a range of experts.

'Use a flash noseband and strap his mouth shut.'

'Use a Plated Pelham'

'Use draw reins to work him in.'

Basically, the advice was to either force his mouth shut or otherwise make it uncomfortable for him to open it – or punish him. Draw reins are particularly tough, giving the rider immense 'leverage' to force the pony into an 'outline' during schooling. It was also not uncommon to see some of the ponies ridden in Tom Thumbs, Swales and even the Sam Marsh bits – perhaps more suitable for bolting hunter cobs – and others with their mouths strapped up tight with flash nosebands.

I asked myself – what is Bear trying to tell me when he opens his mouth? I wasn't about to take away his means of expressing his concerns by strapping his mouth shut, or introducing a severe or restrictive bit – or forcing him to submit with draw reins. We were fortunate that Sam, our show rider, also agreed that we should stay with the lighter bits and careful, positive training approach. She too wanted to see him come to it willingly and retain his sparkle.

However, it was becoming increasingly obvious that Bear preferred riding bitless. While team chasing, cross-country, show-jumping and endurance allow bitless bridles, dressage does not, nor do most shows. Yet around the world, awesome dressage and classical riding are increasingly being performed with bitless bridles – and even with no bridles at all, just a simple cordeo around the neck. I began to discover a world of frustrated bitless riders who yearned for the rules to change.

Both the natural horsemanship and traditional equestrian worlds place much emphasis on the use of a whip – albeit in different ways. Various liberty trainers also use whips. Whichever way you look at it, 'as an extension of your hand', to 'guide the horse' or 'to back up the leg aids so as to remain light with your heels' – a whip constitutes negative reinforcement of your requests. A whip in the hand is also vulnerable to moments of frustration or coercion – humans are humans and bruised egos are fond of whips. A tap with the whip gets results, there is no doubt about that. It gives clarity to your instructions to the horse. However, the whip is saying, 'you MUST do this,' not 'please will you do this.'

In horse agility competition, I did not carry a whip. I'd also now dispensed with the show cane for

Above: Bear going very nicely with Sam at a show

Left: Bear was relaxed and responsive riding out in his Australian Lightrider bitless bridle

Opposite page, top: Even in the best possible hands Bear was showing some resistance to the mildest bit when competing

Middle: Whips are routinely used in the equestrian disciplines

Bottom: Bear hack out bitless

From top: Bear and Sam Roberts stand Overall Ridden Champion at Dunster Country Fair Exmoor Pony Show; Nick, Dawn and Sam with a relaxed Bear at Dunster Country Fair

in hand showing. When I rode Bear out hacking, I sometimes carried a whip as a fly swatter and to open gates, or redirect invasive vegetation away from us. In liberty schooling, I sometimes used a whip as a 'baton' to give extension to my hand, and at other times, I just used my fingertips. This year of ridden competition, where whips were carried in all disciplines, was making me think hard about how and why we use whips generally with horses and ponies.

Out hacking Bear was happy, relaxed and forward-going the majority of the time – and he felt safe and connected in his bitless bridle. I just wasn't seeing the same enthusiastic Bear in ridden competition – even when he had some of the best and most sensitive hands in the business on the reins. I would point out here that the skills of Sam are exemplary – she is the most incredible rider. This was a matter of achieving willing two-way communication with Bear and motivating him to *want* to give his best performance. He was not a 'clock-work' ride – nor did we expect him to be as a fully working stallion with his tempestuous nature and forthright opinions. Producing the best ridden performance from Bear would require patience and understanding and it looked like it would be a long-term job. A ridden, working, multiple-hot-branded, moorbred Exmoor stallion was still a rarity in the show ring.

A Trip 'Up Country' for a Qualifier

One ridden qualifier required us to travel a fair way up country requiring an overnight stay. Bear was stabled in the American barn, which was a considerable change from his usual free-ranging routine with his mares. Early the next morning I took him for a walk where he could graze and enjoy some fresh air on a bridleway adjacent to the arenas. With the grooming basket in one hand and Bear in the other, he meandered and grazed while I prepared him for the show, with the rope draped over his neck. He was relaxed and happy, despite being in a strange place and away from his mares.

Back in the hustle and bustle of the show, the centre was soon teeming with exhibitors and Bear took it all in his stride. However, in the class, I once again noticed him opening his mouth in the Pelham and although producing a nice show he didn't shine in the class. What was required to excel at ridden showing and what Bear responded well to had certainly created a paradox with his ridden development.

Dunster Country Fair – Ridden Champion

This popular Westcountry horse show has its own dedicated Exmoor pony competition, with Exmoor in hand, ridden and working hunter classes and championships. Sam Roberts was able to make time in her schedule for Bear and we decided to return to the simple loose ring snaffle and single rein. He warmed up well and found himself with some stiff opponents, including a fellow breed show winning pony and a rider who had also been to HOYS and Olympia. Today Bear and Sam excelled and he stood Ridden Champion. It was good preparation for the forthcoming Exmoor Pony Breed Show where there would be a Horse of the Year Show qualifier.

Bear relaxing with Nick at the NPS Summer Championships

The NPS Summer Championships

At the National Pony Society Summer Championships, Bear performed well in the Championship Finals he had qualified for. Competing with Dartmoor, Shetland and Exmoor finalists, he finished second in the Intermediate final and fourth in the Open final. His general demeanour at this busy show was exceptional. At one point, I left him with Nick, who took him along to the outside café to get a coffee. When I returned, Nick was relaxing at his table with Bear standing (dozing) quietly beside him on a loose rein. It was hard to believe he was a fully working stallion who had only the day before left his mares and foals.

The Exmoor Pony Breed Show and HOYS Qualifier

Bear was entered for the HOYS qualifier at the breed show and we were looking forward to it. However, the day before the show we wondered whether our show rider needed to be a member of the Exmoor Pony Society in order to ride him there. We should not have worried because as long as a rider is a member of the National Pony Society (which of course she was) they could compete in all HOYS qualifiers without having to be a member of individual breed societies. Nevertheless there was much uncertainty on the day before Bear was allowed to compete.

In the class itself, there was much discussion and poring over the markings between the conformation and ridden judges before the results were announced – which saw Bear awarded third place. He had been given a curiously low conformation mark of 35 out of 50 – for a pony who had twice stood breed show in hand supreme champion and won an in hand NPS Mountain and Moorland gold medal rosette, where top level conformation is essential. It was a day to forget.

Top: Ridden by Sam Roberts

Above: At the Exmoor Pony Breed Show

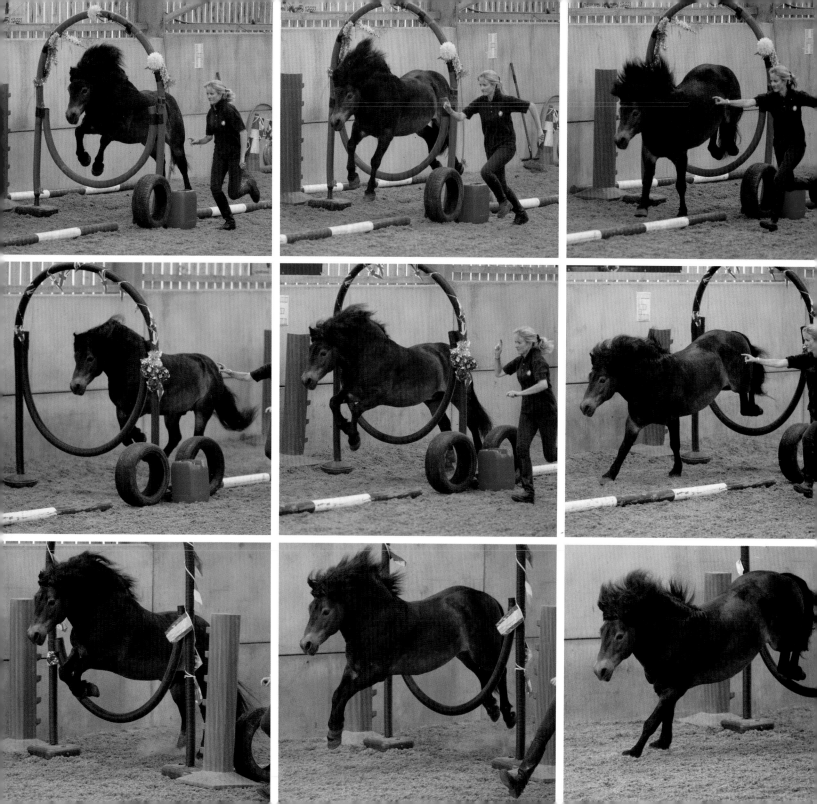

The Exmoor Pony Festival

In early September, we hosted another Liberty and Agility Demo with Bear for the Exmoor Pony Festival and once again, it was very well attended. This year, we'd been working on a Triple Hoop Jump. I'd be asking Bear to navigate a Scary Corner, then move smoothly from walk to canter, jump the three hoops and return to me calmly. To achieve this in front of an audience, we needed a solid connection. After walking into the Scary Corner, he moved into canter and bounded effortlessly down through the line of hoops jumps, then came back to me. It was vital for Bear to be able to manage his energy (and adrenaline) levels as the audience included children, who reached up to stroke his face over the barrier. He behaved impeccably. The important thing was that I remained completely quiet and calm when people clapped – because I was his place of safety. We repeated the Triple Hoop Jump ridden and then everyone watched Bear return to his herd. The festival week once again highlighted and celebrated the many attributes of the Exmoor pony.

Opposite page: Bear navigating the Triple Hoop Jump at his Liberty and Agility Demo

Above and left: Bear accepting a flag over his head, pushing the giant ball and navigating the plastic curtain

The Pivotal Moment

The next show proved to be pivotal for us. After a lovely go around, Bear produced what was probably his best extended trot of the season on the rein change and then, right in front of the judges, came to an abrupt halt – to relieve himself. The determination with which Bear purposefully managed to maintain this halt was considerable, especially with a rider accomplished at maintaining pace and flow. Sam eased Bear on and he continued at a good pace to complete the class. Once again, he appeared to be making a point in his inimitable Bear way.

At the show, Nick pointed out a young pony ridden in a bit more suited to a bolting hunter cob, with what looked like a sore back – indicated through 'dipping' under the rider, a stiff and awkward way of going and an alarmingly swishing tail. I pondered how the end result of rosettes could possibly be worth putting a pony through it and the dulled expression told me it wasn't.

I realised that I massively valued Bear's confidence in expressing his feelings. While this didn't always result in exactly what we wanted, as had been demonstrated in his class today – he reminded us that his tremendous spirit was fully in tact and he had retained his mischievous, characterful sparkle. I wanted to work with him as a willing and enthusiastic partner – not drill and dominate him to do our bidding.

When the apparently sore pony was in the ribbons, I looked at Nick, having reached another milestone.

'This is nonsense.' I said. 'What are we doing here?'

On our return home, the double bridle and Pelham were cleaned and put away in the cupboard. I went out to see Bear in his field, happy with his herd and he came over to greet me.

'Thank you for everything this year Bear. Now you can enjoy a wonderful holiday being a stallion running with your mares.'

He was strong, well-muscled, enthusiastic, fresh and full of presence. He was not showing soreness or wear and tear. Although he had been to a fair few shows, he hadn't been drilled or dulled. We had been fortunate that his show rider was one of the very best in the business and we had not been tempted to over-bit, over-train or over-compete him. He had retained his priceless 'sparkle'. Bear was 'work in progress' and I was not prepared to win at all costs. His wellbeing was paramount. I felt we had more to learn about how to inspire and motivate Bear before we returned to ridden competition. Now, I needed to take stock and think about how and why we were competing – and for what purpose.

It was also becoming increasingly apparent that our energies and focus with regard to Exmoor ponies were needed elsewhere. For the time being, Bear had done the most fantastic and versatile job and he had been working and competing hard for years. He thoroughly deserved his holiday.

Opposite page: Bear demonstrating ridden agility

Chapter 15

Big Developments for Exmoor Ponies and the Story of The Highwayman

Establishing the Moorland Exmoor Foal Project

Along with hot branding, we had become increasingly aware of problems in satisfactorily registering and finding opportunities for wild-born Exmoor pony foals.

Bear – and the other ponies – were doing a phenomenal job in showing us and others how charismatic, intelligent and trainable the moorland Exmoor ponies are, when given a good start in life. Now our attention was being directed to the plight of foals who weren't getting a chance at all.

What was emerging from talking to our fellow Exmoor farmers was that there appeared to be worrying gaps in the 'bridge' that took free-born foals from the moor to good homes. The moorland farmers have a constant balancing act in maintaining the required numbers of their small (endangered) breeding herds and preserving the purebred bloodlines – and finding opportunities for foals each autumn.

We read newspaper articles about moorland farmers who were distraught at the delays in the Exmoor pony registration system, warning that they would result in the slaughter of foals (Ref: *North Devon Journal* and *West Somerset Free Press* – autumn 2013). In some cases, we found that farmers were being discouraged from putting foals forward for inspection at all. Significant numbers of foals were being excluded from registration and there was a worrying amount of culling. Yet the Exmoor was an endangered breed. Something appeared to be wrong.

Vet Peter Green BVSc CertEO MRCVS had been commissioned by the Exmoor National Park Authority and Exmoor Moorland Landscape Partnership to produce a report on the moorland herds of Exmoor – 'The Free-Living Ponies within the Exmoor National Park – their Status, Welfare & Future'. His findings, presented in late 2013, concluded that improvement and change were needed to successfully safeguard their future.

Nick and I wanted to do something to help. We had some useful skills and the facilities to help both foals and the farmers – various of whom were becoming increasingly exasperated. We launched

Above: Moorland Exmoor Foal Project arrivals in 2013 – Farleywater Lady Stumpkin Pumpkin, Firestar and Scarlet

Opposite page: Dawn with Monsieur Chapeau (lying down) Farleywater Dazzler and Farleywater Lady Stumpkin Pumpkin in 2015

Bear awarded WSRC Most Versatile Horse or Pony for competing in show-jumping, dressage and agility

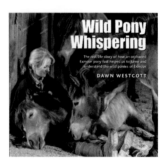

Best-selling *Wild Pony Whispering*

the Moorland Exmoor Foal Project and that winter, helped a significant number of moorbred foals from various herds. This included taking twelve quality foals from one herd who would otherwise have been slaughtered due to obstructions in the registration process.

Riding Club Recognition

At the local West Somerset Riding Club Awards in December, Bear won the award for the most versatile all-round performance horse or pony – with his liberty and agility achievements, ridden showing, dressage and show jumping skills – and achieved fifth place in the Club's annual show-jumping league.

The Events of January 2014

A number of memorable and pivotal events relating to Exmoor ponies occurred in January 2014 which made it an extraordinary month...

The Rescue of Monsieur Chapeau

In the middle of January, we rescued the starving, orphaned wild foal Monsieur Chapeau from the Dunkery Commons, who has brought insight and wisdom to our pony socialisation and training. The immense and immediate trust he gave us has been enlightening for the foal project. This is well documented in my book *Wild Pony Whispering*.

A Positive Breakthrough in the Campaign to Stop Multiple Hot Branding

It was announced in January that a new DEFRA Code of Practice for the Identification of Semi-Feral Ponies was being introduced to make it clear that only free-living foals should be hot branded. With up to four branded marks on the rump still permitted, this was still a considerable way off from a more humane single branded mark. However, the practice would now cease for domestically-born foals, or those leaving a free-living situation. Guidelines were also given for better handling and treatment of ponies. A huge break-through in equine welfare had been achieved. Special mention must be given to Lord de Mauley and Baroness Mallalieu for their efforts.

January 2014 – The Establishment of the Moorland Exmoor Pony Breeders Group

Following the Peter Green consultation and his 'Free-Living Exmoor Ponies within the Exmoor National Park' report, a group of Exmoor farming families and landowners, including the Bryants, Darts, Coldicutts, Floyds, Miltons, Souths, Westcotts (ourselves), Wyatts, Exmoor National Park

Authority – and subsequently the Williams (Molland Estate) – decided to form the Moorland Exmoor Pony Breeders Group (MEPBG). Its purpose was to safeguard the purebred as well as pedigree moorland Exmoor pony genetics and work to improve communication, breeding practices, moorland management, marketing and opportunities for the ponies. The farmers asked Nick Westcott to Chair the group. The MEPBG has since evolved the Heritage Exmoor Pony Register to provide a means of recording, recognising and tracking purebred ponies. Requests have since been made to the breed society to include a supplement and upgrading system within the existing Exmoor Pony Stud Book – and to embrace DNA whole genome testing to confirm purity of ponies. This would provide the structure and process to enable 'unregistered' purebred Exmoors and their progeny to route back into the pedigree breeding gene pool, therefore stemming genetic wastage.

Nick and I were also asked to join the new Exmoor National Park Authority Exmoor Pony Breed Steering Committee, which was formed following the Peter Green report, to progress an Action Plan to improve the situation for Exmoor ponies in Exmoor National Park.

Safeguarding the purebred Exmoor pony genetics was a priority – there were entire moorland herds to assist, including ponies running on Molland Moor and Brendon Common. This included the tiny amount of remaining genetics of the moorland stallion, The Highwayman, from Herd 23 on Anstey Common. Bear himself would play an important role in this.

The Highwayman

Anstey Common and Withypool Common are home to the ancient Herd 23 Exmoor ponies, owned by the Milton family. This is the oldest family owned herd of Exmoor ponies in the world, made famous by Mr Fred Milton who managed them for some decades. Back in the 2000s, Anstey Common had grown wilder than usual, with overgrown gorse making it difficult to gather the ponies. For a few years, this meant that colts stayed out on the moors, with a significant number of entire males competing for the mares. After Fred Milton passed away, Herd 23 was taken over by his great-nephews Rex and Robin Milton, who gathered the common and sorted out the ponies. It became clear that one particular young stallion had fought his way to the top to dominate the herd. His name was The Highwayman and he was regarded by experts as one of the best moorland stallions ever seen. He bore the scars of many fights, and as it turned out, had successfully covered many mares. Keen to register the beautiful progeny, the Milton family put the stallion forward for inspection for a stallion licence.

DNA parentage verification for Exmoors had recently been introduced as a registration requirement for moorbred Exmoor ponies. However, relatively low quality DNA tests were used, which at times could not easily distinguish between the closely-bred ponies. The perils of this along with mis-reading hard-to-decipher hot brands; taking multiple DNA samples without micro-chipping mares; and various admin, data-collection and data-capture errors and mix-ups were not fully realised. Into this medley came The Highwayman and his stallion inspection. He passed the physical inspection with flying colours and was moved to an in-ground enclosure until his DNA was verified

Top: Free-living Herd 23 mares and foals

Centre: The Tippbarlake herd of Brendon Common

Above: Lady Martha of Molland Moor (front left) with the Moorland 99 Herd

and he achieved fully registered stallion status. After which, the plan was to return him to the moor. His progeny were also held at the farm, awaiting DNA parentage verification and pedigree registration. A few foals were sold with the promise of their correct paperwork following on. Amid this period of confusion, The Highwayman tragically got himself hung up in a perimeter fence while trying to escape, and died.

After many months of DNA delays, the breed society regretfully informed the Milton family that The Highwayman, and therefore his progeny, could not be pedigree registered – as the DNA results were inconclusive. The foals were regretfully sent for slaughter by the distraught herd owner who said it had been one of the best year's progeny he had seen. However, with none of the fillies able to join the Exmoor pony breeding herd, and no buyers wanting to purchase non-pedigree ponies, there were no opportunities for these beautiful foals. Almost all of The Highwayman genetics were eradicated – apart from those very few foals who had been sold, and a filly kept by the Milton family to breed from, despite the lack of pedigree registration.

It was a heart-breaking story. All that effort by The Highwayman in becoming the dominant stallion out on the moor and proving himself with exemplary form. Only to be thwarted by administrative red tape with almost total loss of his genetics. Here, man's interference appeared to be aiding the demise of the truly wild moorland Exmoor pony, rather than respecting 'survival of the fittest'.

Anstey Princess – Daughter of The Highwayman

Bear was enjoying his free time immensely. Rolling in mud, snoozing under the trees, galloping about in the pasture, hanging out with his mares and watching the world – it was wonderful to see him relaxing and being a pony.

A thrilling surprise arrived in February while I was pondering which mare to run with Bear in the coming year. A notice was posted on our Exmoor Pony Club facebook page announcing that a mare was for sale as the owner had become frustrated trying to register her. I telephoned to find out more and almost dropped the phone when told that the mare, called Anstey Princess, was by a stallion called The Highwayman. She'd been purchased as a foal with the promise that a pedigree passport would shortly follow. However, this had not turned out to be the case. After years of trying to sort out the situation, the mare was now for sale through no fault of her own.

'I'm coming to see her,' I said. Her owner expressed surprise that we would actually visit and view ponies in ads placed on our social media.

'No,' I said. 'This is not about the advert – I'm bringing the trailer with me. She's sold.'

I think it was only a day or two later that we took the trailer, hoping to purchase Anstey Princess. After asking Rex Milton about her dam, it was confirmed that she was out of a very good registered Exmoor mare called Prince's Golden. With a mother of that quality and sired by The Highwayman, Anstey Princess sounded like she thoroughly deserved her name. But I hadn't even seen her yet. On arrival at the yard, the beautiful Anstey Princess came over to say hello, studying me with the most regal, proud eyes and there was an immediate connection between us. I could not believe we had found her.

'I will look after your daughter of The Highwayman and we'll see if you can have a foal with a sire your father would wholeheartedly approve of.'

Thanking a rather perplexed owner profusely for letting us buy her 'unregisterable' Exmoor mare, we returned home with our precious cargo.

Anstey Princess Joins the Holtball Herd

As it was February, it was too early to put Anstey Princess in with Bear, so she was introduced to the main herd for a couple of months. This proved to be somewhat dramatic. 'Bonnie' had a noble demeanour – calm and dignified and not quick to temper. However, she would also not defer to anyone and this sent some of the other mares into a frenzy. She defended herself with gusto but would not initiate any aggression. It took some very careful introduction over a couple of weeks, and finally the herd found balance again.

Bear Meets Anstey Princess

When the time came for Anstey Princess to run with Bear, I had to separate him from his mares, Maisie and Georgia, who both needed a breeding rest. Georgia's foal wasn't born until they had been separated; however, Maisie's lovely colt foal, Holtball Prince Kailash enjoyed a few weeks with his father. He had been born under a powerful red moon during a total eclipse and this auspicious event inspired us to name him after the sacred mountain in Tibet, Red Kailash. Georgia produced a lovely filly who we named Princess Karisimbi, and they were joined by Jenny and her beautiful filly, Princess Khaleesi. It is fair to say that Bear had his work cut out with Anstey Princess. It took some considerable efforts at seduction on his part to win her over and then they bonded strongly.

Later, a visiting mare arrived and Bear had plenty to occupy his mind that summer. We were thrilled to have the opportunity to help safeguard the genetics from The Highwayman. The Milton family continue to breed quality Exmoor ponies from their daughter of The Highwayman and we all remain hopeful that the stud book will one day include a supplement and upgrading system to enable these valuable moorland genetics to re-join the pedigree breeding gene pool.

Opposite page, from top: Anstey Princess; and with Bear

Above: Joining the Holtball Herd was somewhat dramatic

Right: Bear had to work hard to win the affections of Anstey Princess after which they formed a strong bond

Chapter 16
The Discovery of Wild Stallion Farleywater Zeus and a New Show

The Discovery of Farleywater Zeus

In May, we received a call saying that some yearlings, who had evaded being rounded up the previous autumn, had been gathered in from the moor and had nowhere to go. When we went over to collect Tom Faggus and Annie Ridd, there in the yard was a stunning five-year-old wild stallion, who was identified as Farleywater Zeus. It would later turn out that both Zeus and Annie Ridd were out of a mare called Amethyst.

Zeus was in a predicament. He was a registered and branded Exmoor pony, but not a registered stallion. The clever colt had kept out of sight and had managed to evade the gatherings in the previous few years.

'Can you do anything with him?' I was asked. As I looked at him, Zeus effortlessly jumped from his pen, over the five bar gate into the next penned area.

'Er, I don't think so,' I said regretfully, 'We have nowhere to contain him!'

'Why don't you get him inspected and licenced as a stallion – so his foals can be registered too?' said Nick. And that's what happened.

Farleywater Zeus passed his stallion inspection and returned to the moor to run with a neighbouring herd. The following year, Zeus's new herd had to be re-located. After some consultations amongst the MEPBG farmers, the mares joined the Tippbarlake Herd and Nick and I collected Zeus and took him to his new home to run with the Porlock 100 herd on Porlock Hill. We found a small group of mares and unloaded him and it was magical to watch him meet his new herd. Over the next few days, he patrolled every square inch of his new moorland area and rounded up the mares until he had all of them together again. Previously, little pockets of mares had been grazing far apart. This offered a interesting insight into the impact on herd dynamics when a stallion runs with the mares.

A New Show Emerges

The Moorland Exmoor Pony Breeders Group organised a new Exmoor pony show in August, which is documented in the *Wild Pony Whispering* book. The show was featured as part of the 2014 Exmoor Pony Festival calendar. This year, there was no Liberty and Agility Demo with Bear and putting our

Farleywater Zeus

A very chill wind

efforts into the new MEPBG Exmoor Pony Show with the other farmers seemed to be the best way of making a positive contribution. Importantly, the new show allowed unregistered Exmoor ponies to compete along with Pedigree-Registered ponies – with the respective champions going head to head for the Supreme of Show.

The enthusiasm, support and resilience of our fellow Exmoor farmers was heartening. Working together through the breeders group, we were starting to see extensive improvement in the management and promotion of free-living Exmoor ponies in Exmoor National Park.

The Creation of the Heritage Exmoor Pony Festival

An intensive autumn and winter saw us working to full capacity with the Moorland Exmoor Foal Project, Holtball Herd 11 and our farming. Bear remained 'on holiday' running with his mares. As well as practically helping foals, part of our work was to promote and market moorland Exmoor ponies looking for good homes and we started discussing possible Exmoor Pony Festival events with the other farmers.

However, in early 2015, it became apparent that the festival we'd helped to establish in 2012 had been taken over by a new festival trust, which was unwilling for the Moorland Exmoor Pony Breeders Group and Moorland Exmoor Foal Project to be involved.

As a result, the MEPBG farmers decided that a new Heritage Exmoor Pony Festival should be created and it proved – with hard work and some generous helpers – to be a success that August. The Exmoor farmers, landowners and their supporters had shown once again that they could stand strongly together for the good of the ponies.

Above: Bear could now go to the new MEPBG Exmoor Pony Show

Right: The new Heritage Exmoor Pony Festival

Chapter 17

Bear Meets Wild Mares and the Ultimate Connection

Where to Go Next?

At the beginning of 2015 I contemplated what to do with Bear this coming year. At eleven years old, he was in his prime.

Should we return to competition, concentrate on liberty and agility activities or do something else? There were logistical considerations – not least the time resource available. We now had our hands full to the brim with the management of the Moorland Exmoor Foal Project and Holtball Herd 11 ponies. All this was, however, enabling us to benefit from fantastic learning opportunities in herd behaviour, body language and equine communication – inspiring us to 'go softer' still in our interactions and handling of the ponies.

Bear Returns to Run with Wild Mares

When the possibility arose for Bear to run with some semi-feral mares and spend some time away from home, living wild and free in the valley of a moorland farm, it was not a difficult decision to make. This would be a wonderful adventure and breeding opportunity for him. He would be living in an area with steep and challenging terrain, river and streams, dense woodland and a herd of selected semi-feral mares used to living wild on the moor. Most exciting of all – the mares would then return to their moorland enclosure where Bear's foals would be born the following spring. This seemed like the perfect opportunity for Bear and for the breed.

Bear's Visit to Farleywater to Meet his Wild Mares

The day came to take Bear to Farleywater. The South family had gathered their wild mares and selected some for Bear to run with. Farmer Ian South and his daughter Kate ride out on horseback and quietly gather the mares from about 1000 acres of moorland adjacent to Brendon Common. Then

Bear meeting the semi-feral Farleywater mares; Bear returned to connect with Dawn bringing a wild mare with him, before going back to the herd

they bring them across the 3000 acre expanse of Brendon Common – where the Tippbarlake Exmoor ponies run as well as the moorland cattle and sheep – and make their way down to Farleywater Farm.

For this project, Kate South was in charge of selecting the mares she wanted to include in the breeding programme with Bear. We drove into the yard, met Kate and her mother Helen and then led Bear on the long walk down through the valley where he would meet the mares. It was a fantastic natural environment for the ponies. I took off Bear's head collar and walked with him at liberty – he stayed with us and it was a wonderful feeling to explore the new terrain with him alongside. When he saw the mares, he took off down the incline to greet them. He knew how to behave and also how to impress them and it was amazing to see his display of the kind of moves we can only dream about achieving ridden. Clearly, he was going to get on well with the mares. We watched for some time and as we eventually walked away, I felt so happy for him, but also a wrench at leaving him there.

'We'll be checking them every day, more than once a day!' reassured Kate. I knew he was in good hands – both Kate and her mother Helen adored Bear. He was also familiar with Kate through her time helping with the Moorland Exmoor Foal Project.

Above: Bear reconnecting with Dawn to go home

Opposite page: Bear returns to Holt Ball and his mares and meets Hawkwell Penelope Pitstop (by Ebony)

The Ultimate Connection

It was about a week before I could return to see how Bear was getting on and Kate and I went out to find him. We spotted him way down the valley – and he saw us. He was with the mares, and with one in particular. What happened next brought a lump to my throat. He made his way up the steep hillside to the track, bringing the mare with him. Then he cantered along the track towards us, the mare following behind. As they got closer he slowed to a purposeful trot and the mare stopped a little way off, staring intently and probably wondering why he was so confident in directly approaching us. He came up to greet me and the warmth of the connection was palpable.

After a while, he looked at me and I realised it was time for him to return to his mares. He took the patiently waiting mare back down the valley to join the others.

This wonderful warm greeting happened each time I visited Bear during those weeks. On the day we came to collect him, he left the mares, walked back up through the valley and loaded with no problems. He knew it was time to go home. Certainly, Bear had enjoyed the most amazing adventure at Farleywater.

We had travelled a full circle, my wild stallion and me. Bear had come from a free-living herd to join the world of humans and he'd overcome his fear of contact to build a bond of trust, before returning to run with wild mares – yet willingly choosing to retain our connection. It was indeed like a circle – endless, strong and eternal. For me, that connection between horse and human is what it's all about – it is the ultimate connection. When you let your horse go and he wants to come back to you. No rosette, trophy, prize or title is worth more than a horse who truly wants to return to you – and especially a wild-born Exmoor stallion.

Bear Returns to Holt Ball

When Bear returned to Holt Ball, he was reunited with his original mare Maisie and has been introduced to the inimitable and characterful Hawkwell Penelope Pitstop, who was also born on the moor and sired by a Herd 4 stallion called Ebony. Watching him greet them, newly returned from the Farleywater mares, proud and magnificent, was a sight to behold.

Anstey Princess, daughter of The Highwayman, with her
precious filly foal, Holtball Black Bess, by Hawkwell Versuvius

A Precious New Life, a New Stallion Parade, a True Champion and the Essence of Wild Stallion Whispering

A Bonnie Princess – Black Bess – and Monty's Last Foal

In spring 2015, Anstey Princess produced the most beautiful filly foal, who we have named Holtball Black Bess, in honour of her grandfather, The Highwayman.

The MEPBG established a new parade to showcase Exmoor stallions

Negotiations continue with the breed society to include a supplement and upgrading system in the stud book and embrace DNA whole genome testing, and meanwhile, Holtball Black Bess will be included in the MEPBG's Heritage Exmoor Pony Register.

Holtball Herd 11 also saw the arrival of another beautiful filly foal, Holtball Princess Cristal, by Bear's son Monty. Princess Cristal is Monty's last foal as we had made the difficult decision to geld him in 2014. However, Monty has been given another very important role. He has joined the large herd of Moorland Exmoor Foal Project and Holtball ponies where he runs with mares, geldings and his daughters – who he is very close to. His quality of life in a large sociable herd is one he would never have had as a stallion. When Monty was backed to saddle as a four year old stallion, the whole process was completed quietly, willingly – and bitless. Monty had been well prepared with agility training beforehand and when it came to putting a saddle and rider on, he took it all completely in his stride. He is, of course, not hot branded and neither are his daughters.

The 2nd MEPBG Exmoor Pony Show and a New Stallion Parade

In August 2015, the MEPBG farmers and landowners added an Exmoor Pony Stallion Parade to the MEPBG Exmoor Pony Show at Brendon Show. As the free-living moorland stallions are generally wild and unhandled we were not expecting a large parade. However, Tippbarlake herd owner, Nigel Floyd,

decided that he would like to parade his moorland stallion, Tippbarlake Jamie. This posed quite a logistical issue as nine-year-old Jamie has lived wild and free on the enormous expanse of Brendon Common for his entire life, with various periods in ground when necessary. Nigel felt he could make the necessary connection with Jamie to enable him to be exhibited at the Stallion Parade. I would be taking Bear and Nigel's daughter Jess would be taking her new two-year-old colt, Waltersgay Nutcracker.

After a morning waiting in the trailer while we showed some young ponies – the characterful Monsieur Chapeau, Imperial Topaz and Lady Molly of Molland Moor – the first thing Bear saw when he came down the ramp were the unhandled moorland mares and foals in their pens. As this pioneering show's rules allowed it, I had decided to show Bear in the bitless bridle.

Bear was keen to go and see the mares and foals and the merits of the **Core Connection Warm-up Exercises** became apparent – being able to gently disengage his hind quarters, draw him back to me and ask him to turn and lead away from the mares – without having to haul on the rope or cause jarring on his jawbone from a bit in his mouth. As Bear took in the show ground and the bustling atmosphere, he channelled the energy he'd accumulated waiting in the trailer into some impressive leaps. A few years ago, my own adrenaline would have shot up. Now I knew that when Bear needed to let off some steam, he required me to be as cool as a cucumber. He would 'come down' when he could. I breathed and gently invited him to walk with me. He began to focus and lower his adrenaline. It felt really good. The consistent work socialising the foals, especially following the arrival of Monsieur Chapeau, had brought me to a new level of understanding – and softness – and in turn this was enhancing my partnership with Bear.

Bear and I walked across the far end of the show ground and standing there, watching the activity in the rings, was Nigel Floyd with his moorland stallion, Tippbarlake Jamie, who was on a loose lead rein. The majestic wild stallion was

Left: Staying calm while Bear let off steam was essential

Below: Bear watching the show

Bottom: Wild moorland stallion Tippbarlake Jamie with Nigel Floyd

wearing a simple head collar, relaxed and ears pricked. It was a sight to behold. Given the free-living background and lifestyle of Jamie, it was incredible to see him standing there happily with Nigel. No stallion bit, no chain, no whip, no leaping, fighting wild stallion. Just a sense of peace, purpose and pride – on both their parts.

The MEPBG Stallion Parade was in the main ring and all three stallions behaved impeccably. There was a good crowd of spectators and Gethin Rees, the local auctioneer, gave a commentary on the background of each stallion – it was a wonderful publicity opportunity for Exmoors. So after almost two years away from showing, Bear had returned to parade. It was good to be walking next to our beautiful stallion again.

Above: Bear's very first moorbred Farleywater foal, born in April 2016

A Roller Coaster of a Decade

The past decade has been a rollercoaster ride – with highs and lows and much in between. We've tamed and produced a top quality wild-born Exmoor stallion, enjoyed success in the show ring, won two world championships in horse agility, launched the Moorland Exmoor Foal Project and helped to form a proactive breeders group which has seen the coming together of Exmoor farming families, experts and authorities to safeguard important genetics. This includes the establishment of the DNA Whole Genome Project Team, of which I am part. With stakeholders including Exmoor National Park Authority, The Rare Breeds Survival Trust, the MEPBG, the Exmoor Pony Society, Grassroots and Peter Green, working with Nottingham University and Chaired by DEFRA Chief Vet, Tim Morris, this offers a fantastic opportunity to define, map and safeguard Exmoor pony genetics.

There has been the development of a connection with Bear and the other ponies that I could only have dreamt of when I brought home Harry, my first Exmoor pony. Once a petrified and touch-resistant colt foal, Bear has achieved performance levels that have caught the attention of horse people across the globe. In the past decade, I've competed and then questioned the very essence of competition, yet not lost belief in its merits or purpose.

We've stood up against Multiple Hot Branding which has required strength and resilience to deal with. However, the required welfare improvements have begun to take place – and are continuing.

All of this has offered lessons, opportunities and a steep learning curve on many levels. One poignant lesson learned is that just because something has been done for a long time, it doesn't necessarily make it right. Above all, it has taught us to never, ever give up, to stand up for what you believe is right – and that adversity can be overcome.

A True Champion for the Exmoor Pony Breed and the Essence of Wild Stallion Whispering

This whole experience – and having the privilege of sharing life with Bear – has shown me that while competition is a worthwhile part of the journey, there is more. What counts is each and every moment and whether your horse is happy and able to do what you're asking him to do – enjoying a willing partnership and striving for harmony. We'll endeavour to work with people and organisations that respect the evolution of the horse as our trusting friend, not simply as an animal to control and do our bidding. Certainly, we look forward to continuing to work with great riders like Sam Roberts.

The emphasis for us is learning how to engage the ponies trust, enthusiasm and interest – making the effort to understand and listen to them, through respectful two-way communication. That is the essence of Wild Stallion Whispering and actually, anyone can do it if they want to.

Bear and Nick have shown me that we have a much bigger job to do in Exmoor ponies than winning rosettes – we need to keep building that vital bridge from the moor to good homes for wild moorland foals like Bear, so they get the opportunity to show us what amazing, intelligent, capable and charismatic ponies they are. Yet winning rosettes and showcasing the attributes of the ponies has its value and importance in promoting the breed. The Exmoor is endangered and its future will only be safeguarded if people continue to take an interest in the ponies, particularly with regard to the wild foals of Exmoor National Park.

Bear has proved to be an incredible ambassador for Exmoor ponies, demonstrating their qualities to the world in so many ways. Conquering his initial fear of humans, allowing himself to trust us and showing such an aptitude for performance – as well as the way he has handled his roles as a working

stallion and father to his foals, and shown courage in overcoming adversity. He has contributed a tremendous amount to our understanding not only of wild Exmoor ponies, but stallions generally – stripping away fears, prejudices and frequent misunderstandings of these awesome equines. Stallions can be safe, kind, loyal, loving, fun and sociable – even when completely at liberty in wild, wide open spaces, and running with mares. He is still fresh, full of presence, charisma and enthusiasm – and there is more to come. That, in my mind, makes Bear a true champion of his breed – and of the world of the Horse.

It also highlights Exmoor ponies as some of the world's greatest equine teachers – both in horsemanship and with regard to our own evolution and self-development. Bear, I take my hat off to you.